"Scott Kiloby's Living Inquiry practices, pa [barcode] Inquiry and the others he teaches in this bo see that the more we believe our thought, and life to be reality, the more unhappy and lost we become. Through his simple and elegant technique of Living Inquiry, Scott helps us to find the natural rest and peace of our true nature in the simplicity of this present moment. He shows us how to navigate the often confusing relative world of emotions, relationships, roles, and human functions, with the wisdom and peace of the absolute perspective. This book is a masterpiece of skillful means for living everyday, ordinary, human life with wisdom and grace. I highly recommend it."

—**Francis Bennett**, author of *I Am That I Am*

"'*It's just a movie!*' This statement summarizes a major theme Scott Kiloby interweaves throughout his book, *The Unfindable Inquiry*. He describes the movies that are too often playing inside our mind... As Kiloby rightly points out, most people never stop to inquire, '*Who is this "me" that is watching and identifying with these movies?*' When we do inquire, as Kiloby expertly guides us to, we can come upon the astounding conclusion that this 'me' is actually a timeless presence that is spacious, perfect, and whole—beyond border, boundary, and lack....

"Kiloby shows us simple and elegantly designed exercises that liberate us from our core wounds, which show daily on our internal screens as movies of self-deficiency and blame, victimhood, and other-blaming. He enables us to recognize and 'rest' as the spacious, compassionate presence that we truly are and have always been, which we've simply forgotten but can now remember through his expert guidance....

"Kiloby provides us with the means that can liberate us, truly, into a lifetime of freedom, joy, well-being, and interconnection—within ourselves, with others, and with the world around us."

—**Richard Miller, PhD**, clinical psychologist, spiritual teacher, and author of *iRest Meditation* and *The iRest Program for Healing PTSD*

"This book, and this work, changed my life. I was so unhappy with who I was, constantly seeking for something better, for the bliss of enlightenment to take me away from myself, because being me was so painful. *The Unfindable Inquiry* helped free me from my longing to be something other than what I am. This book offers a profound, life-changing experience. It's not enough to read it and try to understand it. It must become a regular practice. It must be lived to reap the full benefits. If it's real freedom you're after, this book and the tools it offers are an indispensable guide."

—**Julianne Eanniello**, assistant director of
The Kiloby Center for Recovery, Inc.

"Scott Kiloby's Living Inquiries and Natural Rest are powerful tools that have changed my life. The basic method is simple and easy to understand. We hold a lens up to our experience and inquire into thoughts and feelings that cause suffering. Scott gives clear examples of how to free ourselves from identification and limiting core beliefs in *The Unfindable Inquiry*. He then takes the basic inquiry and shows us practical ways to transform our daily lives through going deeply into topics like bullying, perfectionism, abandonment, seeking, anxiety, and control. There is value here for us all."

—**Lynn Fraser**, senior facilitator and trainer of
The Living Inquiries, http://nondualinquiry.com;
and meditation and yoga teacher certified in the
Himalayan tradition, www.stillpointyoga.ca

"Scott has a gift for expressing the deepest and most profound concepts in simple and easily understood language. He is able to do this without losing any of the depth and nuance of what is being addressed. I have always found Scott's writings inspirational, and this book is no exception. In *The Unfindable Inquiry*, he offers practical and effective counsel that provides the reader the opportunity to meet each moment as it appears, and therefore inquire directly into the cause of their suffering. This has the potential to transform our everyday experience, allowing us to live more authentically and joyously. I enthusiastically recommend this book, and in fact, all of Scott's writings."

—**Paul Galewitz**, certified facilitator of The Living Inquiries, www.authenticinquiry.net

"I recommend Scott's book *The Unfindable Inquiry* to many clients, and use it for all my Living Inquiry courses. Scott writes for people of all backgrounds and ideologies, in such a way that it is easy to read, easy to digest, and easy to put into action. His invitation to look and journey inward is rich and profound. I highly recommend this book to anyone who wants to get to know themselves and their experiences."

—**Lisa Meuser**, senior facilitator and trainer of The Living Inquiries, www.integrativehealingnow.com

"Inquiry has been practiced for centuries in a variety of contemplative traditions. Generally, such practices were done by advanced yogis and monks, reserved for the few. The Living Inquiries helps make this form of practice simple and accessible for all of us, here and now. Any belief, perceived problem, or source of suffering can be worked with. The Living Inquiries and the Unfindable Inquiry, in particular, have been a real blessing for me, and I am extremely grateful to Scott for having had the chance to learn and practice them. I highly recommend them to anyone who would want to go deeper and experience more freedom."

—**Greg Ascue**, senior facilitator and trainer of The Living Inquiries, www.restingawareness.com

"*The Unfindable Inquiry* is a brilliant and life-transforming guidebook to understanding how life works—how we try to mold it to fit our needs and desires, and suffer as we fight against reality. Life has its own path and unfolds in its mysterious ways. After years of meditation to learn to quiet my mind's disturbing thoughts and beliefs, I was still perplexed in everyday life, especially in relationships. Once I found Scott Kiloby's teachings and began inquiring with curiosity into my thoughts and beliefs, the confusion began melting away. Now, in my seventies, I am reseeing my life with a wiser perspective, as I have come to understand what Scott describes as 'the middle way'—somewhere between the human self that can feel separate and alone, and the self that is part of the larger whole and can appear as empty. *The Unfindable Inquiry* facilitates an unwinding or untangling of confusion that brings relief, resolution, and peace. I am immensely grateful for the opportunity to work with my own beliefs, and for my certification as a facilitator of the inquiry process, which allows me to help others."

—**Judith Sumitra Burton**, certified facilitator of
The Living Inquiries, www.awakeningfreedom.org

"This book is an easy-to-read, practical guide on how to use the Unfindable Inquiry in your daily life. A myriad of problematic areas (e.g., conflict, perfectionism, bullying, helping, control, seeking), all common to our human lives, are described from a revolutionary angle. Each problematic area comes with a clarifying dialogue, between the facilitator (Scott) and a client, that helped me understand the flow and the structure of the Unfindable Inquiry. Because of the repetitive character, I also got the hang of doing self-inquiry by reading them....

"I can honestly say that the Unfindable Inquiry has changed my life: patterns (e.g., the need to please) are falling away; resistance is almost gone. There's a basic trust now that all that happens can be embraced, and that it is healing to do so. I can rest, letting myself be guided by life. From this place, I'm able to meet others and myself, just the way we are, and feel compassion for all of us, including myself."

—**Hanneke Geraeds-de Vries**, facilitator, www.stress2balance.nl

The
UNFINDABLE
INQUIRY

ONE SIMPLE TOOL TO OVERCOME FEELINGS OF UNWORTHINESS & FIND INNER PEACE

SCOTT KILOBY

NON-DUALITY PRESS
An Imprint of New Harbinger Publications

Publisher's Note

This publication is designed to provide accurate and authoritative information in regard to the subject matter covered. It is sold with the understanding that the publisher is not engaged in rendering psychological, financial, legal, or other professional services. If expert assistance or counseling is needed, the services of a competent professional should be sought.

Distributed in Canada by Raincoast Books

Copyright © 2016 by Scott Kiloby
    Non-Duality Press
    An imprint of New Harbinger Publications, Inc.
    5674 Shattuck Avenue
    Oakland, CA 94609
    www.newharbinger.com

Cover design by Amy Shoup

MIX
Paper from
responsible sources
FSC
www.fsc.org   FSC® C011935

RAINFOREST ALLIANCE CERTIFIED

Library of Congress Cataloging-in-Publication Data on file

18 17 16

10 9 8 7 6 5 4 3 2 1   First Printing

Contents

The Sense of Core Deficiency

Todd and Traci are on the train, heading home from downtown after a night out. Traci's nose is buried in her latest find from a secondhand bookstore. Todd, sitting next to her, can just see the first words of the title: *Good Health Is a Matter of....* He smirks. He can't make out the last few words, but he assumes that the book is about self-improvement, as usual. And Traci, if she noticed that familiar smirk of his at all, keeps on reading as if she hasn't seen it.

Earlier, they had dinner at their favorite restaurant. Todd ate his usual big plate of lasagna with a serving of steaming-hot garlic bread. Traci, already stuffed to the gills with sloppy spaghetti, went on to order dessert, too.

Traci stops reading for a moment and thinks: *Why did I eat that chocolate cake?*

Todd begins daydreaming about their favorite vacation spot, a quaint beachfront town on the East Coast. They both adore the quiet, cozy atmosphere of the cottage where they always stay, with the constant splash of ocean waves outside the thick sliding-glass door to the deck. But Todd knows they can't afford to go there this year—he's just lost the job he had for fifteen years—and his daydream turns to worry about their bills and their dwindling retirement account.

Traci's gaze drifts back to the brittle yellowed pages of her book. She sees the words "Many people have difficulty losing weight as they grow older."

Todd turns to her and says, "Wasn't that meal fantastic?"

Traci, feeling insecure about her bloated belly, answers brusquely: "We can't afford to eat there as often as we used to."

Todd feels so bad about losing his job that he can't help taking Traci's remark personally. Irritated, he fires back. "What's that," he says, pointing to Traci's book, "another self-help masterpiece you'll stop reading halfway through?"

What Traci hears is *You're fat and ugly, Traci*. "Don't worry about my books," she snaps. "At least *I* still have a job to pay for them."

From here, they jump headfirst into a rapid exchange of insults, each spouse targeting the other's deepest insecurities. And after ten years of marriage, they both know just the right buttons to push. What follows is their routine of mutual silent treatment as each nurses the hot sting of the other's words. For the rest of the ride home, Todd and Traci privately replay their old mental scripts.

As the two of them lie down to sleep, Todd's thoughts are spinning with a familiar story of financial insecurity and unworthiness. Traci lays her head on her pillow and listens yet again to the nagging voice in her head that tells her she's unattractive and unlovable. She fixes her eyes on Todd. *He can be so cold sometimes*, she says to herself. *Who did I marry?*

Meanwhile, Todd might as well be a million miles away—he doesn't even notice Traci's lonely stare. Powerless to stop his own rapid-fire thoughts, he has traveled back to a past that seems to confirm his unworthiness. Overwhelmed by fear, he finds himself blaming Traci. *She doesn't understand what I've been through*, he tells himself. *She doesn't support me.*

The Core Deficient Self

Somewhere along the way as we go through life, often in our early years, we begin to believe a lie about who we really are. And the lie sticks because we unconsciously repeat it to ourselves as we grow into adulthood. I call that lie the story of the *core deficient self*. It arises from the part of our identity that continuously creates the core story of who we think we are.

This false story comes in many forms, but it's usually a version of *There's something wrong with me*. It's a lie through and through because there actually is no core deficient self at all, and so the story can't be anything more than a set of thoughts—that's all. The story seems true, though, because we believe it.

Todd's story of unworthiness and Traci's story of unlovability are their personal variations on the story we all tell ourselves about the core deficient self. When you believe your own version of this story, you experience a deep and corresponding emotional wound in your body, a wound easily reopened in relationship. You may not know that there is a wound within you. You may not realize that you believe, at the most basic level, that you are deficient. Quite often you don't even see your story, but you still operate and react from it. That's because the story, to one degree or another, remains not fully conscious.

Exchanges like the ones we just saw between Todd and Traci are all too common. We long for harmonious relationships, but we often come up short and find conflict instead. Even when life seems to be flowing smoothly, a core story lies dormant within. Like a fearful snake coiled up and waiting to defend itself, the story (along with its corresponding emotional wound) strikes when others push the right buttons. Its venomous bite leaves you spiraling down into self-judgment and doubt, and then it's fight or flight all the way—you either attack and defend or you run and hide. Your reactions are often intense, too, as if you were instinctually fighting or running as a matter of survival. And why not? After all, the very foundations of your human identity are challenged when an emotional wound is reopened in relationship.

Facing a core emotional wound can seem way too scary for most people. Even when you momentarily have the confidence to look more closely at your story of core deficiency—for example, when you want to free yourself from its grip—what you often find yourself doing instead is reconfirming your story. When your wound is reopened and your story of core deficiency is triggered, your mind scrambles to understand what's happening and to grasp who you are in relation to others. But the scrambling takes place in the same mind that created the story in the first place.

When you're using a search engine, you never find any information that isn't already in its database, no matter how many times you click the search button or icon. In much the same way, when someone reopens an emotional wound in you, and you consult your mind for information about how to react, you're often pulled right back into the same loop of thought that you've always known. Again and again, your mind reconfigures itself along the lines of a familiar script: *There's something wrong with me.* The story of the core deficient self is much like a stone wedged solidly into the earth. You can polish or mask the stone's surface, but unless you dig the stone all the way out, it stays stubbornly embedded. In the same way, you can add new lines to your script, and you can use therapy, positive affirmations, or other interventions to improve your core story, but unless you confront your core emotional wound and see through your story of the core deficient self, that story will remain embedded in your identity throughout your life, endlessly reasserting itself one way or another in all your relationships.

Did you notice how Todd and Traci slipped into the automatic response of pointing outward, toward each other, as soon as their emotional wounds were reopened and their stories of core deficiency were triggered? That's what we all commonly do, to protect ourselves from having to face the emotional pain that accompanies our stories about the core deficient self. We unconsciously trap ourselves in the fight-or-flight response. If you don't have the right tools to free yourself from the grip of your story about the core deficient self, it's easier and safer to point away from it. Facing it directly is just too much.

The less willing and able you are to confront your core story of deficiency and its accompanying emotional wound, the more you'll point outward to keep from having to look within, and this outward pointing is what will keep you continuously blind to the inner lie that something is wrong with you. The story of your core deficiency constitutes a blind spot because you can't see your story as long as you're pointing away from it. When you protect the story of your core deficient self instead of facing it and seeing through it, you unconsciously feed that story, and then you blame others for your emotional pain instead of taking responsibility for what you've come to believe about yourself. (That's not to say that you don't also blame yourself sometimes, too, further strengthening the story about something being wrong with you.) You point outward from your blind spot, and that outward pointing fuels your emotional pain, which in turn fuels your need for more self-protection and self-preservation, and those needs produce still more outward pointing. It's an insidious, vicious cycle, and it's something we all unconsciously do to ourselves. That's why it really hurts.

Deficiency and the Belief in Separation

When we're very young, a basic sense of separation begins to arise in us—the feeling of a clear distinction between *me* and everything that is *not me*. Life becomes a play of separate objects in relationship to each other, and the main object is *me*. That sense of separation is appropriate when we're very young. Treating our bodies as separate is a matter of instinctual survival, just like finding food, clothing, and shelter.

But in early childhood, the instinct to survive expands beyond basic physical matters and comes to include the psychological and emotional realms. As we identify ourselves with words, mental pictures, emotions, and sensations, they appear to us to be welded together, and they come to make up the belief, in each of us, *I am a separate person*. For each of us, somewhere along the way, all those words, mental pictures, emotions, and sensations—the elements of the belief *I am a separate person*—become attached to a deficiency script, the story *There's something wrong with me*, and this attachment marks the birth of the inner lie, the story of the core deficient self. In this way, our belief in our own separateness is directly tied to our belief in the story of our core deficiency.

As we deepen our belief in our core deficiency, we become convinced that love, validation, security, completion, approval, importance, worthiness, and other desirable qualities exist outside ourselves, and we long for the wholeness we lost when we came to believe that we're separate from others. And so, trapped in the vicious cycle of pointing outward, away from our deficiency, we also begin to *look* outward, seeking in vain for whatever it is that seems to be missing inside. For example, if we think that our parents didn't fill the gaping hole inside us, or even that they created the hole in the first place by not giving us what we needed when we were children, then we spend the rest of our lives trying to fill it through our later relationships. And that's only natural.

But by the time we're adults, our belief in our core deficiency is driving many of our actions, in our relationships as well as in life as a whole, and so we find that everything we've come to believe about ourselves is mirrored back to us by others, *precisely because we bring our core (deficient) identities into every relationship.* For example, if my story of core deficiency is that I am invalid, then you will appear to confirm that story in me. If your story of core deficiency is that you are unlovable, then I will appear to confirm that story in you. Then, instead of looking directly at our belief in our separateness and deficiency, both of us will point outward, toward each other: "You are the problem, not me!" This is how we'll get locked into mutual affirmation of our stories of core deficiency, and how we'll stay blind to that inner lie as well as to our sense of being separate from each other. And as we experience hurt, invalidation, abandonment, insecurity, rejection, incompletion, or disapproval in relationship, our sense of separation will be strengthened, and we'll continue searching outside ourselves for what we think is missing, never truly and permanently filling the hole we perceive inside us, continuously strengthening the story of our core deficiency.

On some level, though, you know that if you begin to go inward and directly confront the pain of being separate and deficient, your belief in your core deficiency will begin to crumble. Your carefully constructed personal story of core deficiency will fall apart. And what this dissolution of your story brings up is your fear of death. Your deepest fear, your fear of losing that deficient core identity, keeps you locked in the cycle of focusing on others instead of challenging your notions of who you take yourself to be. This fear pulls you back into the mind, with all its familiar words and pictures telling you that you're separate and deficient. And so relationship becomes something of a well-oiled machine, one that's perfectly designed to keep you locked into the false story of who you are.

Even when you begin to see that your belief in being a separate, deficient person lies at the heart of your struggles in relationship, you may not have the right tools to see through that false story. Without effective tools, you'll tend to rely on your mind, which will usually send you back into the story of your deficiency, and back into the automatic response of pointing outward, away from your pain. This book provides very effective tools for helping you see through the story of your core deficiency by showing you how to focus directly on the emotional wound that lies at the heart of that story. By facing the wound head on, you are freed from its grip.

My Non-Dual Realization and My Work with Others

Some years ago, I experienced a profound realization that my identity as "Scott" and my belief in being a separate person were illusions of mind. In other words, I came to see that individual separateness is not real, and that I wasn't who I'd taken myself to be. These days, this type of insight is generally referred to as a "non-dual realization," or an awakening. My awakening released me from a lot of suffering and futile seeking as my urges and efforts to change myself, others, and my present experience began to quiet. The profound feeling of peace and love that washed over me has stayed with me ever since, and the initial insight that I experienced has continued to deepen.

In the early days, I was very eager to help others come to the same realization I'd had because it brings such contentment and well-being. I began meeting with people in private sessions and in groups, and as the years went by, more and more people came to me for help. Some were spiritual seekers on the quest for enlightenment. Others were just looking for freedom from suffering around issues like addiction, anxiety, and depression. Still others, constantly on the road to self-improvement but never reaching a place where they felt complete, were tired of merely trying to change their stories of core deficiency or their lives. Traditional therapy and other approaches had already failed many of them, and they felt a deep longing to wake up from all the mental stories that for most of their lives had been such a constant companion and source of suffering.

Some sessions were with people who still clearly believed in their separation as individuals, and who told me about the suffering, useless seeking, and conflict that accompanied their struggles in relationship with other people and with things. Other sessions were with people who had already experienced some degree of awakening but were still affected by some version of the core story *I am deficient*. Over the years, however, I noticed that even if someone claimed to have awakened, it didn't matter much—very often, the core deficiency story was still quite active in relationship, often in unconscious ways. The sessions could be intense—some people sobbed as they told me about lost loves, childhood traumas, failed romantic relationships, sexual abuse, addiction, anxiety, fruitless seeking, victimhood, alienation from friends and family, bullying, and many other things. Other people were basically content and relatively free from suffering, but they still reported that something was missing from their connections with people and with the world. In all the sessions, virtually every issue seemed to boil down to the sense of deficiency.

I also met with many spiritual teachers, not in sessions but in casual conversations. These were people who would be considered fully realized by most standards. In quiet moments of honesty, we spoke of how, even after our awakening, the sense of core deficiency continued to arise to different degrees in our own lives. I talked to many students of spiritual teachers, too, and heard disturbing tales about teachers who refused to look at this issue, teachers who claimed to be awakened even though patterns of deficiency were still operating in certain areas of their lives. Those tales were quite revealing. I came to see why there's such a long history of spiritual teachers' involvement in scandals concerning sex, power, control, jealousy, competitiveness, and other issues. What's at work in those situations is the teachers' sense of core deficiency. And, as mentioned, I certainly saw deficiency patterns in my own experience, too, well after my initial awakening. All these circumstances led me to focus even more on the sense of core deficiency in my own life and in my work with others.

The Inquiries

The inquiries in this book are a tool I developed for myself, as a way to penetrate my own leftover deficiency patterns. As I saw how helpful the inquiries were for me, I began using them with clients. While clients experienced the appearance of words, mental pictures, emotions, or sensations, I asked one simple question: "Is that you?" This question was intended to help clients see if they could actually find the "not good enough" self in the deficiency story. And, session after session, the client could not find that self.

The sessions started to change dramatically. Many clients reported newfound freedom, peace, and love in their lives. Happiness no longer felt to them like something they would have to continue chasing into the future. Happiness was revealing itself in their present experience. They began to see that their constant desire to change themselves was actually one of the major reasons for their continued suffering. The inquiries helped them settle into a deep and radical acceptance of life as it is. The sense of core deficiency began to vanish from their experience, and this change positively affected every area of their lives, including their relationships.

The central tool presented in this book is the Unfindable Inquiry. Although this inquiry is often used on stories of deficiency, it reaches far and wide and can be used on any area of human suffering, as you will see. The Unfindable Inquiry has two cousins—the Boomerang Inquiry and the Panorama Inquiry, which are both relationship inquiries—but these two, despite having different names, are not really different from the Unfindable Inquiry; rather, they're tools to help you illuminate and name the story of core deficiency that underlies whatever struggle, conflict, or disharmony you're experiencing in your relationships so you can more easily use the Unfindable Inquiry on that sense of deficiency. Still more inquiries have been developed as offshoots of the Unfindable Inquiry, including the Compulsion Inquiry and the Anxiety Inquiry. The latter two are not included in this book, since they merit separate exposition and explanation, but the Compulsion Inquiry can be found in my book *Natural Rest for Addiction: A Radical Approach to Recovery Through Mindfulness and Awareness*. Together, all the inquiries are referred to as the "Living Inquiries."

There are now many trained and certified facilitators of the Living Inquiries who work with people all over the world—in private sessions and in groups, via one-on-one video chats, on the telephone, and in person. With this book, it's my pleasure to bring the Unfindable Inquiry to the general public. Although you can use the book to begin doing the inquiries on your own, I highly recommend working with a trained facilitator as soon as you can. A facilitator will help you avoid traps and pitfalls and do much deeper work, and afterward it will be much easier for you to continue the inquiries by yourself. You can find a facilitator at http://www.livinginquiries.com or http://www.naturalrestforadd iction.com.

Rest

You'll notice that the thoughts described in this book are sometimes broken down into words and mental pictures, and that emotions and sensations are often referred to as "energy" or "energies." Your belief that you're a separate, deficient person arises when you *identify with* words, pictures, and energies rather than seeing them as temporary phenomena that come and go. When you're suffering, what you're actually doing is taking words, pictures, and energies for objective reality, a reality that includes an objective self, objective others, and other objective things. That's why, throughout this book, you'll see instructions to "relax" words and pictures, which simply means letting them drop out of your awareness. You'll also see the words "rest" and "resting." They refer to a basic capacity within your direct experience—your capacity simply to be in the present moment, just as it is, and be aware of words, pictures, and energies as they appear and disappear. We're all so busy believing in or identifying with the words, pictures, and energies that make up our personal stories that we overlook our more basic capacity to rest not *in* but *as* the thought-free space that's left behind when words, pictures, and energies subside and relax. As you'll discover, however, your basic capacity to rest and allow all words, pictures, and energies to be as they are is central to using the inquiries as a way of seeing that words, pictures, and energies are ephemeral, and that they don't refer to, represent, or reflect anything objective.

The inquiries are designed to help you face and allow painful emotions just to be as they are, and resting helps you use the inquiries. So what is resting, and how do you rest? Stick with this simple approach:

1. Bring your attention to the felt sense of spacious aliveness in your inner body, including your chest and stomach

area, because these two areas are where emotions generally arise and subside. Don't think about or label this alive spaciousness; just notice that it's there. When you do, you withdraw energy from the thought stream, and you rest as thought-free space.

2. Whenever a thought arises, simply notice it. As that thought disappears, bring your attention back to the felt sense of spacious aliveness in your inner body, and rest again as the thought-free space that remains after the thought has subsided.

3. Throughout the day, every day, take brief moments to rest as thought-free space. How brief should these moments of resting be? At first, just three to five seconds at a time. How often should you take these moments of rest? As often as you can. Just return again and again, as often as possible, to that felt sense of spacious, alive presence in your inner body, not thinking about it or labeling it but simply noticing that it's there.

As you engage more and more in this practice, the moments of thought-free rest naturally become longer, and it becomes natural and automatic to rest throughout the day. This practice helps you see that words, pictures, and energies simply arise and subside and don't refer to, represent, or reflect anything objective.

Before you begin doing the inquiries, you may want to spend some time just becoming acquainted with resting throughout each day. I can't emphasize enough that recognizing your basic capacity to rest, and to simply be aware of words, pictures, and energies as they come and go, will help tremendously as you do the inquiries.

CHAPTER 1

The Unfindable Self

The Unfindable Inquiry is the main tool in this book. This chapter provides an explanation of the Unfindable Inquiry. This inquiry sets the foundation for the relationship inquiries—that is, the Boomerang Inquiry and the Panorama Inquiry—which we'll encounter in later chapters, but the Unfindable Inquiry itself is not a relationship inquiry. Instead, it invites you to try to find a particular person (such as "me, the victim") or a particular thing (for instance, "cancer" or "resistance"). As you will see, however, knowing how the Unfindable Inquiry works is integral to working with the two relationship inquiries that you'll encounter later on. All of this will become clearer as you continue reading the book.

The inquiries in this book are based on actual sessions I've had with people. Names have been changed, along with some of the circumstances, to protect the privacy of the individuals involved.

In the example inquiry in this chapter, Caleb is trying to find the victim he takes himself to be. I've done this inquiry with people on just about every identity you can imagine, from father to CEO to worthless self. I've also done the inquiry with people on the basic belief in being a separate self (ego) without putting any additional label on it, like "worthless self." It works well either way. I have to say, though, that the inquiry is most potent when you add a label to it. Just as the word "leaf" doesn't point to any particular kind of leaf in the forest, the word "self" doesn't point to anything in particular, but when you name a leaf a "maple leaf," you know exactly what you are trying to find, and when you add a label to the self (such as "the one who isn't good enough" or "the victim"), you know exactly what you are trying to find— the identity you take yourself to be. We all have different stories that we take ourselves to be, and it's helpful to give a particular label to the content of your story. I think the remaining chapters of the book will make this idea clearer.

It may sound funny to say that you cannot find your self when you try to really look for it, but give the inquiry a try. It may surprise you. Even though it may feel strange to look for something that seems to be obviously there, it is a powerful inquiry. The self that you try to find is empty when you look for it. "Empty" means "unfindable."

The Unfindable Inquiry can be used on anything, not just a self. I encourage you to look for anything that you feel exists in a separate, objective, inherent way. You can look for any person, place, or thing that feels objective. For example, you could look for "my crappy life," "cancer," "death," "awakening," "suffering," "America," "the dining room table," or "my friend Barbara."

How the Unfindable Inquiry Works

1. Name it. Name the person (for instance, "the unlovable self," "the victim," "the one who isn't good enough").

2. Find it. Try to find that person. One by one, go through each of the main words, pictures, and energies that make up the person. For each appearance ask, "Is this me?" Once you ask the question, stop and be directly aware of

each set of words, each picture, each energy, by itself, to see if it is really the person you take yourself to be.

A person is something more than a temporary set of words, a temporary mental picture, or a temporary bodily energy. We conceive of the person as a fixed, objective, separate, and permanent entity. But that's exactly what you can't find when you look.

If you are looking for something other than the self, just change the inquiry to name the person, place, or thing, and then try to find it by looking through the words, pictures, and energies that arise, one by one. Remember, the word "energy" refers to any emotion (sadness, fear, and so forth) as well as to any sensation (tightness, pleasure, pain, contraction, color, shape, sound). Look at everything during the inquiry.

The Unfindable Inquiry: An Example

Scott: Name the person you would like to try to find.

Caleb: I'd like to find me.

Scott: OK, we can do the inquiry on the general sense of self. But sometimes it's helpful to see if there's something specific about you that brings up suffering.

Caleb: I've always thought of myself as a victim. Life treats me unfairly. I'm miserable most of the time. Yesterday is a good example. I just sat around all day feeling alone.

Scott: So let's try to find Caleb, the victim. Relax and make yourself as comfortable as you can. Close your eyes and look at the word "Caleb" in your mind. Take your time. Is the word "Caleb" you, the victim?

Caleb: No, that's just a name, just a word.

Scott: How about the words "Life treats me unfairly"? Is that you, the victim?

Caleb: Is that me? No, that's just a thought.

Scott: Be careful not to answer just with the intellect. Look directly with awareness. And remember to pay attention to your body. Does the body react in some way when you see the words "Life treats me unfairly"?

Caleb: Yes, there's sadness.

Scott: Look directly at the word "sadness." Is that word you, the victim?

Caleb: No. But the thought "Life treats me unfairly" has returned.

Scott: Put the words "Life treats me unfairly" into a picture frame in your mind. That can help you see that they're just words. Now look at the words in that frame. Is that the person who is a victim?

Caleb: No, those are just words.

Scott: Put the words "I'm miserable most of the time" in a picture frame in your mind. Are those words you, the victim?

Caleb: Yes, that definitely feels like me. The sadness is back, along with contraction.

Scott:	Whenever words or a picture seem like you, it always means that some energy—some emotion or sensation—is arising along with it. Emotions and sensations are like alarm bells reminding you to be in your body, and to feel the energy directly. So relax all words and pictures—just let them drop out of your awareness. Relax all words and pictures, and rest. Take your time. Bring attention to the nameless energy in your chest. Let that energy be as it is. Is this energy you, the victim?
Caleb:	That energy feels like me.
Scott:	OK, whenever an energy feels like the self, it just means that some words or pictures are still arising along with it. What is appearing?
Caleb:	The thought "This is me."
Scott:	Frame those words. Are the words "This is me" you, the victim?
Caleb:	No, I can clearly see that those are just words. Now they're gone.
Scott:	Bring your attention back into the body, without any words or pictures. Is that energy you, the self who is a victim?
Caleb:	No, that's just energy. There's no story with it. And the sadness and contraction are disappearing now.
Scott:	Look at the picture of you sitting around yesterday feeling alone. Is that picture you?

Caleb:	I can see that it's a picture, but it feels like a victim. The sadness and contraction came up again.
Scott:	Are the words "sadness and contraction" you, the victim, when you look directly at them spelled out in front of you?
Caleb:	No, those are just words.
Scott:	Be aware of the sadness and contraction, but without naming them. Is that energy you?
Caleb:	No, that's not me. But that energy feels stuck.
Scott:	Whenever energy feels stuck in the body, there's still identification with words or pictures. Sometimes there are mental pictures being projected by the mind onto the sensation or emotion. This makes the energy feel more solid. Close your eyes, and tell me if you see any mental pictures.
Caleb:	Yes, it feels like the energy is contained in a knot.
Scott:	Look just at the picture of the knot. Gently observe the picture, without describing it. You can even bring the picture up, away from the energy, and look at it floating in space. Is that picture you, the victim?
Caleb:	No, I can see it's just a picture, and it just relaxed. Now the sadness is welling up.
Scott:	Relax all words and pictures, and just experience that energy, letting it be exactly as it is. Take your time. Is that energy you?

Caleb: Wow, no! It just moved through. I can see now
           that when no words or pictures are placed on
           emotion, it's not a victim. I don't feel like a victim.

Scott: Just rest now, letting anything and everything
           arise and fall naturally. Can you find the victim?

Caleb: I see a thought here and there, but when I ask,
           "Is that me?" I can see it's just a thought, and it
           disappears. There is an emotion, but when I rest
           into it, it disappears, too. I can't find the victim.
           In fact, I can't find a self. This is so simple and
           effective. I have literally been thinking of myself
           as something I can't find when I really look.

A Few Helpful Tips

Let's go back over this inquiry and add some tips that may help
you. Put yourself in the place of Caleb:

- *Simplify thoughts down to either words or pictures.* If you
  look into your experience, you can see that thoughts
  arise in one of two different ways—either as words or as
  pictures. Words are literally things, such as "Caleb" or "I
  am a victim." Pictures are mental images, such as the
  memory of sitting yesterday and feeling alone, or the
  picture of a body part or a knot. It is good to see the difference between words and pictures. Notice exactly
  which of these is arising to give you the sense of a separate person. It may also be helpful to frame the particular
  words or pictures. For example, imagine the words "I'm
  miserable most of the time" inside a picture frame in your
  mind, or on a road sign. Stare right at the words. Keep

looking straight at the words, and then ask, "Are these words me, the victim?"

- *Refrain from trying to answer the question "Is this me?" intellectually.* Notice that I asked Caleb not to answer intellectually. Don't think about your answer. Don't analyze the question. Don't refer to other parts of your story to find the answer. Just look directly at whatever is appearing, by itself, whether it's a set of words, a picture, or an energy. Look at it in the same way you would look at a color without naming it—directly, with bare naked observation. From that direct observation, ask, "Is this me, the victim?" Intellectually, you may understand that words or a picture are not the person (victim). But these inquiries have nothing to do with an intellectual understanding. When you are looking at words or pictures, pay attention to your body. Notice when the body reacts with an emotion or a sensation. This is the body's way of letting you know that, on some level, you believe that you are those words or that picture. Notice that Caleb intellectualized when I asked him if the thought "Life treats me unfairly" was him. After he mentioned that he felt sadness and contraction along with that thought, I encouraged him to pay more attention to his body.

- *Keep your answer to the question "Is this me?" to a simple yes or no.* Don't add detailed analysis to the answer. For example, if you are truly a victim, and if that victim is here, present in and as your body and your mind, then it shouldn't be hard for you to find it. You should be able to find it right away, in your direct, present experience, without the need for elaboration. Take the example of looking for a pair of shoes in a closet. If you pick up a shirt, there is no need to give five reasons why the shirt is not the pair of shoes. You know that it isn't the pair of shoes. No elaboration is needed; you just keep looking for the shoes. Treat this inquiry the same way. Stick to simply trying to find the person, with a simple yes or no.

- *Remember that you're looking for the person, not for evidence of the person, or for thoughts that point to the person, or for parts of the person.* During the inquiry, it may seem as if every set of words, every picture, and every energy you encounter is "part of" the person, is evidence of the person, or is pointing to the person. Don't settle for this kind of thinking. Go deeper. Look for the person itself. If all these temporary things point to it, then where are *you*—the real, permanent, separate, actual victim? If all words describe it, then where are *you*? If these appearances are merely part of it, then where are *you*? The *you*—the actual victim—is what you're looking for. That's what is unfindable when you look for it directly instead of thinking about it. For example, if you're looking for the victim you take yourself to be, then it may seem as if the words "Life treats me unfairly" are part of the victim. Forget about finding parts. Look for the victim itself. Are the words "Life treats me unfairly" *you*—the actual victim? That's the proper question. We often assume that these kinds of thoughts are describing or pointing to an actual, inherent victim that is really there, underneath the thoughts. To prove that the victim is not there, underneath the thoughts, just drop—relax—any thoughts that seem to describe or point to the victim. Notice that if you relax these thoughts, you can't find the victim when you're directly looking for it. But you can't find it when the thoughts are there, either. You find only thoughts, one after another—no actual victim.

- *If you're looking at words or at a picture, and if the words or the picture seem to be the person, then this always means that there is some energy, some sensation or emotion, arising with the words or the picture.* If the body reacts in any way to the question "Are these words me, the victim?" just say, "Yes, this is me." Then bring your bare attention immediately into the body, and experience the energy directly, letting it be exactly as it is, without trying to change it or get rid of it. If you find your mind labeling the emotion or sensation with words such as "sadness" or "contraction," ask yourself, "Is the word 'sadness' me, the victim? Is the word 'contraction' me?" If not, then relax all words and pictures for a few seconds, and experience the energy without any words. Simply rest with the raw sensory experience itself. And then ask, "Is this energy, by itself, me, the victim?" If you see that it is not the person, then let it be as it is, without trying to change it or get rid of it. This frees up the energy to move and change naturally, and it often dissolves. But the point is not to try to get rid of anything. That's just more seeking. The point is to see that the energy is not the person. Once you see that no words, no picture, and no energy is the person, it no longer matters as much whether these things arise. Any appearance can come and go, yet the victim is never found. This allows the story and the emotions to quiet naturally and effortlessly. Suffering, seeking, and conflict show up in our experience from our unconscious belief that these appearances form a separate person.

- *If an energy—that is, an emotion or sensation—in the body seems to be the person, this always means that there are words, pictures, or both words and pictures arising along with the energy.* If this happens, notice the words or pictures that are coming up with the energy. Then look directly at those words or pictures and ask, "Is this me, the victim?" An energy seems like the person only when words or pictures are arising along with it. Pay particular attention to those subtle mental pictures, such as images of body parts and other forms and shapes in the body, that appear to contain certain emotions and sensations. If you see a picture when you're experiencing energy, then ask whether that picture, by itself, is the person. For example, is this picture of a knot the victim? You can even imagine a frame around the image, if that will help you see that it is only a mental picture, not a person. Observe the picture directly until it begins to change on its own or disappear. As you see that these are just mental pictures, and that they are not the person, the pictures tend to change or disappear on their own. Even if they stick around, it won't matter as much, once you see that they are not the victim. Don't skip the mental pictures that may arise around emotions and sensations. They are very important in these inquiries.

- *See that words, pictures, and energy are not actually welded together.* When you think you are a separate person, notice that words, pictures, and energy seem welded together. For example, when the words "I'm a victim" arise, it can feel as if the emotion of sadness is welded together with the words, and that a picture of the stomach, for example, is welded together with the words and the sadness. All three appear at once, as if Velcro were holding them together. This is called the *Velcro effect.* Really pick apart the words, pictures, and energies, and for each one, each time, ask, "Is this me, the victim?" This is a powerful way to untangle the experience of words, pictures, and energy being welded together. When you're not able to find the person in any one of these words, pictures, or energies, and when you allow these appearances just to be as they are, you undo the Velcro effect, and your suffering is released.

Keep It Simple: Three Elements, One Question

If you find yourself overcomplicating the "finding" part of the inquiry, just remember this: three elements, one question. For all the inquiries, there are only three elements to look at—words, pictures, and energy. And there is only one question, stated in different ways:

- Are those words me, the victim?

- Is that picture me, the victim?

- Is this energy me, the victim?

Keeping it simple keeps the mind out of the game. This is a direct looking for a self, or for some other thing.

CHAPTER 2

The Unfindable Others

The Scandal of Believing in Objectivity

Much of the disharmony in relationship can be attributed to the belief in objectivity—that is, belief in the notion that we experience other people the way they really are. As we've seen, the belief in objectivity tends to arise right along with the belief in being a separate individual. Through my own separate *me*, I see separate others. Once you've made this division in your mind, there's a tendency for you to believe that *you*, the subject, can see other people and objects exactly as they are. And in that tendency there's a kind of mental sleepiness, a blindness to the fact that every time you *see* anything, what you're actually doing is *thinking*. You fail to see that you're looking through a filter of thought.

When you believe in objectivity, you have difficulty seeing that your words, pictures, and energies paint others in a way that is unique to you. Your words, pictures, and energies make up your entire view of reality. Your views of other people are shaped by your memories, your personal history, your culture, your worldview, and your psychological and emotional traits along with various other influences. You don't see others the way they are.

You see them the way *you* are. The painter is inseparable from the painting.

For a quick experience of this reality, rest for a moment without any thoughts. In the moment of resting without thoughts, you don't know who or what a person is, *precisely because no thoughts are arising in you.* Your thoughts inform you of everything you think you know about anyone, including yourself. When thoughts begin to arise in you, notice that they're coming from your own personal set of memories. Each of your arising thoughts has to do with a particular past experience, one that you interpreted in a personal and particular way. Your view of another person is actually a view of your own memories, as if you were in a relationship with your memories and not with the other person. And as emotions and sensations arise alongside your memories, your image of that person is reinforced.

Notice that this is always the case, no matter whom you encounter. At any given moment, the way you see a particular person—that is, your thoughts about that person—will depend completely on the particular words, pictures, and energies that are arising in you. And what you think about that person will have a lot to do with your education, your upbringing, your fears, your thoughts about yourself, and many influences from your culture that shape your attitudes about who people are or who they should be. This reality can be difficult to see until you begin meeting people freshly in the moment, without dragging your memories into each encounter and using them to interpret others' words and actions in the present. When you're not able to see that your thoughts are producing your view of another person, you buy into the belief that you are seeing the other person objectively, exactly as he or she really is. You can't see that your view of the other person is relative and subjective. You can't see that your view of that person is limited to what you think, feel, and sense in the moment.

Even though any one of us may know, at the intellectual level, that our view of someone else is subjective, relative, and limited, we often act as if our view of that person were objective. For example, Brad and Tony are discussing the leader of a Middle Eastern country. Brad, a Democrat, finds himself disagreeing with Tony, a Republican. Brad gets very upset as he listens to Tony. Intellectually, Brad may know that his view of the Middle Eastern leader is largely subjective. He knows that his view has been shaped by his experience of being a Democrat and by all kinds of other experiences. But his intellectual awareness doesn't stop him from getting angrier and angrier as he listens to Tony. Brad thinks Tony just doesn't get it. He really wants to prove that Tony is wrong about this leader. The very fact that Brad gets so angry as he listens to Tony is an indication of just how deeply Brad believes that his thoughts actually represent reality. There's nothing wrong with anger. It's a natural human emotion. But it's often based on a skewed view of reality. Brad is acting and responding to Tony on the basis of his own belief in objectivity. The Middle Eastern leader is not just someone who's "out there," separate and objective. Brad and Tony are both experiencing particular thoughts, emotions, and sensations that paint the leader in a certain light—as good or evil, right or wrong. And their emotions will tend to strengthen their particular views and mindsets, making their thoughts seem all the more objective.

The belief in objectivity is a scandal. Look at the degree and depth of the suffering and conflict that have arisen throughout history from the basic belief *I see others the way they really are.* I call it a scandal because this belief is universal, but we don't realize it's a belief. We mistake it for reality, and this mistake comes at great cost, creating widespread disharmony in human relationships. The scandal has left us with a trail of murder, torture, rape, abuse, war, conflict, bullying, divorce, control, manipulation, alienation, and loneliness in relationships.

Whenever we fail to see the subjective nature of our experience, we treat others as objects who are somehow independent of our own thoughts, emotions, and sensations. This belief in objectivity is directly related to our desire to change, manipulate, abuse, judge, blame, bully, and control others, as well as to our tendency to seek approval, attention, self-worth, validation, and love from others.

When we're pointing outward, we're overlooking the projector—the self—that shows the world in a particular way. When we stop pointing outward, when we stop behaving as if we could see people and situations objectively and focus instead on the thoughts, emotions, and sensations that are arising within us, a new clarity becomes available to us. We free ourselves from the belief in a self that sees others the way they really are. And our relationships begin to harmonize. As a direct result, the world "out there" begins to reflect our own inner peace, joy, love, compassion, and wisdom. The inner and the outer become inseparable. Once we see this, we can still express our views, but we can do so without the belief *I see others the way they really are.*

The Unfindable Others

Take a good look at what's happening between you and the people you're close to. For example, imagine you're a man married to a woman who nags you all day, and who can seem cruel when she speaks her mind. It may seem to you that your wife just shows up in front of you each day, exactly that way. The story of who your wife is may even seem to be embedded in her body, and to exist completely on its own, on her side of your interactions, no matter what thoughts, emotions, and sensations are arising in you. You may even find that many people agree with your assessment of your wife. But it's also likely that someone, somewhere, thinks your wife has good reason to nag you, and that her honesty in speaking her mind is refreshing.

The point is this: The wife you experience is shaped deeply by what you think, feel, and sense about yourself. Your perceived wife is influenced by your own needs and desires, your personal story, your family upbringing, and the beliefs of the culture in which you live. This insight doesn't excuse any of your actual wife's behavior. It just sheds some light on your view of her behavior.

When your wife walks into the room, your own memories, conscious and unconscious, flash into your mind. Perhaps there's a memory of a hurtful thing your wife said yesterday, or the memory of how things were when the two of you first met, or a memory of how your mother treated you when you were a child. Memories, when they arise, are often accompanied by emotions and sensations, and so your memories come to seem like a reality that exists "out there," completely apart from you. But others who experience your wife walking into the room don't have your particular memories, and so their experiences of her will probably be different from yours.

The primary thing for you to notice is that you are experiencing inner words, pictures, and bodily energies that present your wife to you in a unique way. You don't have to intellectualize this fact. To see it, just use the Unfindable Inquiry. But this time, don't use it to find yourself. This time, use the Unfindable Inquiry to find the other person.

Can you find your wife? Walk up to your wife, and intimately touch her shoulder, feeling the sensation of soft flesh. Ask yourself, "Is this sensation, by itself, my wife?" Notice that the sensation itself doesn't tell a story. It's just a sensation of softness, by itself. It doesn't whisper to you the word "wife." The word "wife" is just that—only a word.

Is the word "wife" your actual wife? Look directly at the word in your mind, or hear the sound of it in your head, and notice that this word, the sight or sound of it, is not actually your wife. Then look at the more emotionally driven views that you have about her. For example, are the words "She nags me all day" your wife? How about the words "She can be so cruel"? How about your mental picture of her frown? Try to find your wife as an objective, separate person. Are any of these words, pictures, or energies your actual wife? Watch as the next set of words or the next picture appears. If the words or the picture really do seem to be your wife, this just means that some energy, some emotion or sensation, is arising along with the words or the picture. As we've seen, this is the Velcro effect in action. Move your attention to the energy in your body, without labeling it. Is that energy, by itself, your wife? Experience the energy directly until you see that this energy is not your wife. Let the energy relax. Let it fall away naturally. If the energy still seems to be your wife, notice that words or pictures are continuing to arise along with it. Observe each word or picture directly, without judgment, and ask, "Is this my wife?" See that it's only a set of words, only a picture.

In that moment when you can't find your wife except in your own inner words, pictures, and energies, what's actually happening? Is no one there? Is there really no wife at all? That would be taking things a little too far. Yes, there is a wife who appears before you. But your experience of that person you call your wife is not an objective experience. You're *looking at* your wife through a subjective filter. When you *look for* your wife with the Unfindable Inquiry, and when you don't find her, you see that much of what you've been taking to be objectively true about her has begun to relax. Then it becomes easier for you to meet her freshly in each moment, without unconsciously dragging all your thoughts into that moment and looking at her through such a clouded lens.

When you mistake your unique, clouded lens for a clear window on objective reality, you invite misunderstanding, disharmony, and conflict into your relationship with your wife. But greater intimacy, compassion, and acceptance of others begin to appear as you begin to see through your belief in objectivity.

Using the Unfindable Inquiry to Find an Other: An Example

In this inquiry, I helped Tom use the Unfindable Inquiry on his son, Brandon, who had just announced to the family that he was gay. Notice how I pointed Tom in a direction where he didn't have to simply believe whatever he thought. I helped Tom challenge his most deeply held assumptions about his son, and about gay people and women in general.

Tom: My son, Brandon, just told me he's gay, and I believe that homosexuality is wrong. I knew when he was a kid that he was more feminine than other boys. I put it out of my mind. I wanted him to "man up." But he didn't. I'm wondering if I did something wrong, if I didn't father him correctly.

Scott: Can you find your son?

Tom: Yes, he's my son. Of course I can. He's lived with me all his life. I know him really well.

Scott: I didn't ask whether you know him or have lived with him. I asked whether you can find him. Is the word "Brandon" your son, Brandon?

Tom: No, that's just the name we gave him at birth.

Scott:	Is the word "son" Brandon, when you look at the word spelled out or hear it streaming in your head?
Tom:	No, it's just a word.
Scott:	Are the words "Brandon is gay" your son?
Tom:	Yes, that feels like him. And it doesn't feel good at all.
Scott:	Whenever words feel like your son, it just means there's bodily energy stuck to them. This energy is not always conscious. In other words, you aren't directly aware of it as it's arising. So become aware of it now. What emotion or sensation happens when you have the thought *Brandon is gay*?
Tom:	Sadness and a bit of embarrassment, and shame for feeling embarrassed.
Scott:	Is the word "sadness" your son, Brandon?
Tom:	No, that's just a word.
Scott:	How about the words "embarrassment" and "shame"? Are those words your son? Take your time. Really stare at each thought until it begins to fade.
Tom:	No, just words.
Scott:	Then just let those words relax. Let them fall away. Bring attention into your body, and really experience directly what shame and

embarrassment feel like when you aren't placing words on those energies.

Tom: Yeah, I'm feeling that. It feels very uncomfortable. I can see myself wanting to escape these feelings.

Scott: When you aren't labeling that energy in your body, is it your son, Brandon?

Tom: No, those are just feelings.

Scott: Let those feelings relax on their own, as if you had no agenda about pushing them away or making them stay.

Tom: As soon as I felt them, they became more intense. I saw a desire to get out of my body and go back into thinking. But I stayed with them, and now they're dissolving. I can definitely see, on some level, that those emotions were playing into the words "Brandon is gay."

Scott: Are the words "Homosexuality is wrong" your son, Brandon?

Tom: No, I know those are just words.

Scott: Pay attention to your body when you answer. Is your body reacting to the thought *Homosexuality is wrong*?

Tom: Yes, I feel a strong contraction in my gut.

Scott: Are the words "I feel a strong contraction in my gut" your son, Brandon?

Tom: No, those words aren't my son.

Scott:	Drop those words for a few seconds, and experience the contraction by gently observing it. Just notice that there's an inner, aware space in your body. Let that space be aware of the energy without labeling it. Take all the time you need. Is that energy your son, Brandon?
Tom:	Yes. For some reason, that feels like him or closely associated with him.
Scott:	Whenever a sensation feels like someone, it just means there are still some words or pictures coming through. Can you see any words or pictures?
Tom:	Yes. I can't believe I'm about to say this, but what came up was "My manhood is being challenged." Wow, Brandon's homosexuality feels personal to me, to my own sense of being a man. I can see how society has shaped my view about what a man is supposed to be. And that has nothing to do with Brandon.
Scott:	It has nothing to do with you, either.
Tom:	That's a little harder to see.
Scott:	Use this inquiry to look at that belief later. For now, let the words "My manhood is being challenged" fall away for a few seconds. Just look directly at the thought, and watch it disappear. Then feel the energy of contraction, without words and pictures around it. Is that energy your son, Brandon?

Tom: No, and it's not me, either. It's just energy. And I can feel it relaxing now. Funny how I thought that was Brandon, and also that it was me.

Scott: Look at the mental picture of Brandon as a young child, looking feminine in your eyes. Is that picture Brandon?

Tom: It's a picture of him, yes. That's him as a child. I actually try to put that picture out of my mind most of the time. You just brought it up, and I can see that I take that picture to be him.

Scott: Let the picture fall away naturally by just observing it. What emotion or sensation is arising?

Tom: I'm feeling sad and disappointed.

Scott: Are the words "I'm feeling sad and disappointed" your son?

Tom: No.

Scott: How about the energy of sadness and disappointment when you aren't describing it with words?

Tom: Yes, that energy feels like him.

Scott: That just means that some words or pictures are coming to mind again. What are they?

Tom: I'm embarrassed to say this. The thought *Women are weak* came to mind along with the thought *Brandon looks weak, too*. It's incredibly painful to see that I believe this. I must believe this about all women, including my wife.

Scott:	Is the thought *Women are weak* your son?
Tom:	Ha-ha! No, not at all. I can see that this is mostly about me, my ideas around manhood, and even my fear of women or feminine energy. It feels threatening.
Scott:	Are the words "It feels threatening" your son, Brandon?
Tom:	At first it seemed like those words were him, but when I dropped into my body and just felt the fear without calling it fear, it wasn't so bad. It washed away. So, no—the words aren't him. And that energy is not him.
Scott:	Is that energy in your body your wife, or women in general?
Tom:	No, that seems ridiculous now.
Scott:	Look at the words "I didn't father him correctly." Are those words Brandon?
Tom:	No.
Scott:	Take a moment and rest here in the present, letting anything arise, any thought, emotion, or sensation. Can you find Brandon, your son?
Tom:	Not really. I do see a picture of him kissing a man. That feels like him.
Scott:	Do you notice an emotion or sensation arising?
Tom:	Yes—disgust. I'm dropping that word to just feel what disgust is really like when I'm not labeling it.

Let me see…is this energy Brandon? No, it's not him. And when I look back at that picture, I see that's not him. That picture and those feelings have to do with my own beliefs about manhood and homosexuality.

Scott: Can you find Brandon?

Tom: Yes. He's sitting at home right now.

Scott: Is that picture in your mind of him sitting at home your son, Brandon?

Tom: Oh, that's interesting. No, that's just another mental image. I don't even know if he's at home now. I'm seeing something amazing. Everything I've taken to be Brandon is a thought, with emotions and sensations. I'm feeling such great spaciousness now, such peace and lightness around this whole issue of Brandon being gay. I can see that I love him. I mean…I love my story of him. I can see that I've always only had a *story* of him. It's like I've never met *him*. I've never allowed him to be who he is. I only wanted him to be my image of him. And so much of that just came from my beliefs about men and women, and homosexuality. This is such a release of all that.

Incorporating the Unfindable Inquiry into Your Life

It was poignant to watch Tom come to the realization that he was not interacting with his son the way his son really was. He was mistaking inner words, pictures, and bodily energy for an objective, independently existing son. And the words and pictures were largely influenced by his cultural beliefs about masculinity, femininity, and homosexuality.

From the time we're born, we're inundated by the prevailing beliefs of the culture in which we live. Those beliefs define and shape who we are, and who we think others are. When we look at others, we're often looking at our own projections and fears. But that's not obvious until we start looking directly at the words, pictures, and energy that arise and fall within us.

Now that you've seen the Unfindable Inquiry being used in this way, you can take it into your own life. How do you see your husband, your mother, your boss, your neighbor, your government leaders, your friends, and your enemies? For each person you encounter, look directly at the thoughts that arise within you. Do the inquiry. Notice the extent to which your emotions and sensations play into what you believe about someone. Don't analyze. Just use the Unfindable Inquiry to find the other.

The Unfindable Inquiry can be used on many levels of our human experience. Imagine government leaders using the Unfindable Inquiry on other government leaders as they contemplate going to war. Imagine a rapist using the Unfindable Inquiry before he acts on his impulses. Imagine an angry mother using the Unfindable Inquiry before she lashes out at her child. Imagine the political pundits on TV using the Unfindable Inquiry before they begin ranting and raving about what's wrong with the world today. All it takes to use the Unfindable Inquiry is being open to looking in a different way instead of immediately believing your thoughts to be objectively true. And if you consider the long history of suffering that humans have experienced with each other in relationship, you'll see how much we could use a different way of looking.

CHAPTER 3

The Deficient Self in Relationship

The Core Deficient Self: A Believable Illusion

Now that you've seen how the Unfindable Inquiry works, let's take a closer look at relationship, and at how the belief in a core deficient self drives so many of our actions and reactions when it comes to others. The deficiency story is like a false script, one that tells a fundamental lie about who we really are, a script that we carry around from childhood into adulthood. It's directly related to the belief in being a separate person. In reality, there isn't a deficient, separate self; we just believe that there is. The deficient self comes in many forms—the unlovable self, the weak self, the powerless self, the inadequate self, the unacknowledged self, the abandoned self, the invalid self, the unimportant self, or some other version of the stories *I'm not good enough* or *There's something wrong with me.*

When I first started writing books, I didn't mention the core deficiency story. That was because, back then, I couldn't see how pervasive the story really is. But once you start to look, it's everywhere. The world practically runs on the story *There's something wrong with me.* Our relationships are often controlled by this central belief about ourselves.

I had seen this belief in myself through the years, but I didn't have a name for it. I couldn't see how deeply it was operating in me until I began using the Unfindable Inquiry. Once I started using the Unfindable Inquiry on myself, I began to see this basic belief, *I am deficient*, as the trunk of a tree that has many branches. The branches are thoughts like *I need to change, I wish I could be more like him, I'm not successful enough yet,* and *She doesn't like me.* I noticed that if I focused only on the branches, trying only to decide whether each thought was true, I would find myself swirling in a bottomless pit of self-analysis and would never get to the root belief in a core deficient self. But once I started to follow all those branches back to their trunk—a single deficiency story, which for me was *I'm unlovable*—the whole tree began to come into view. I knew then that whenever I was triggered in relationship, in any way, all I had to do was try to find that unlovable self. What made all the difference was focusing on the trunk instead of trying to cut down all the branches.

Relationship Is a Mirror

Relationship has a built-in mirroring effect. As you move through life, it seems as if other people reflect the core deficient self back to you. When the wound that lies at the heart of the deficient self is reopened, you experience pain and suffering. No one else has actually reopened the wound—that's a misconception—but it hurts all the same, and that pain is responsible for much of the difficulty you experience in relationships. If the pain gets too intense, you may find yourself trying to avoid it, blaming others for it, or medicating it. Like everyone else, you have a tendency to believe that others are the source of the pain. But others are just a mirror showing you what you believe about yourself.

Here are a few signs that the core deficiency story has been activated in relationship:

- Insisting on being right, and making others wrong

- Excessively seeking love, praise, attention, acknowledgment, or approval from others

- Comparing yourself to others, and judging yourself as better or worse

- Belittling, ridiculing, or bullying others

- Trying to control or manipulate others

- Recoiling fearfully from conflict when it would be more authentic to speak your mind

- Judging others negatively, or complaining about them

- Expressing anger and other emotions in unhealthy, destructive ways

- Alienating yourself from the people around you, and avoiding certain painful relationships

- Acting on selfish ambition

- Suppressing painful emotions, and not expressing how you really feel

- Feeling jealous or envious of others

Much of this mental activity comes from being afraid to look directly at who you've falsely taken yourself to be. But others in your life are constantly mirroring back to you this illusion of a core deficient self.

If you look closely, you'll see that the mirroring effect is operating in every direction. When you view others as successful, what is often mirrored back to you is an unsuccessful self. When a loved one doesn't respond to you in the way you expected, or when a romantic relationship ends, what is often mirrored back to you is an unlovable self. When you judge certain people to be important in the world, what may be mirrored back to you is an unimportant self, or an unworthy self. When someone judges or criticizes you, what that judgment or criticism may mirror back to you is a self that feels wrong. When others appear arrogant or authoritative, what their attitudes may mirror back to you is a weak, insignificant, or small self. If others appear powerful, you may feel less powerful, or even completely powerless.

And this mirroring effect doesn't just operate with other people. Anything can mirror deficiency back to you. A drug addiction or problems with money may mirror back to you a self that is lacking. The conscious or unconscious memory of past traumatic events may mirror back to you the sense that now, years later, you're still a victim. Future goals like enlightenment, recovery, and self-improvement may mirror back to you a self that still seems incomplete.

This kind of mirroring doesn't always amount to a simple play of opposites. The outer circumstances of your life, no matter what they are, generally reflect something about how you view your self. If it seems to you that your outer circumstances are inadequate, then you may also be experiencing yourself as inadequate. The point is that inner and outer are one—whatever appears to be going on "out there" reflects, in some way, what is actually going on "in here," in your self's identity.

Pointing outward at others through the mirror of relationship means, in the most basic sense, looking to people and things outside yourself for your self-esteem. Whenever you believe that true, stable, permanent happiness depends on other people or on the outer circumstances of your life, you're deriving your self-esteem largely through the mirror of relationship, and you're setting yourself up for disappointment. If your positive view of yourself is based on comparing yourself with others, or on expecting yourself to measure up to a particular set of desirable outer circumstances, and if those people or outer circumstances should happen to change for the worse, then your inner view of your self may quite easily start to seem deficient again. Not everyone is deeply unhappy all the time, of course. To claim such a thing would be to insult all the people who are living happy lives right now. But identities based on mental stories and images are unstable. That's why this book focuses mainly on the negative self-identities that seem to stand in the way of genuine happiness.

As the inquiries in this book reveal, true self-esteem has nothing to do with mental stories and images. It has nothing to do with defining yourself through the mirror of relationship. True self-esteem arises out of selfless presence—out of your ability to rest as thought-free space, your capacity to experience yourself and others freshly in the moment instead of believing that your mental stories and images are showing you the world and other people as they really are. True self-esteem comes from your ability to see through your story of the core deficient self. That's why true self-esteem cannot be destroyed by the thoughts and actions of others.

The Panoramic View

To get a better view of how deeply the way you move and act in relationship may be affected by a belief in your core deficiency and your separateness, try this:

1. Imagine yourself sitting in the middle of a room, with all the other people and things in your life placed around you in a circle.

2. Scan around the whole circle.

3. As you look at each person or thing, notice how it appears to reflect back to you the idea that you are deficient in some way.

This panoramic view will help you see and name the particular deficient self that you take yourself to be.

When you believe that you're deficient at the core, the people and things in the circle seem to confirm this belief. Everything and everyone can act as a trigger for the core belief *There's something wrong with me*.

But there's also another possibility. Look around the circle at each of the people, and see if you experience yourself as being inherently better than some of them—as if your essential nature contained a brightness that's absent from others in the circle. If so, then you'll come to see, when you're deeply honest with yourself, that your only reason for believing you're inherently better than others is your feeling of being deficient at the core. You can hide that feeling of deficiency by overcompensating with the mind, by creating a false sense of self to hide the deficiency from others and from yourself. You can falsely prop yourself up. But then, because of this false sense of self, you'll never be able to know yourself except in relation to others—you will never appear without reference to others. If you take yourself to be better or more worthy than others, then you won't be able to sustain that superior identity unless you're around others who appear to be worse or less worthy than you.

The Benefit of Seeing Through the Core Deficient Self

As you experience freedom from the belief in being deficient, it becomes naturally easier for you to move, act, and respond more selflessly and confidently in relationship, with a clear mind and an open, fearless heart. You don't have to cultivate these qualities or put on an act about being loving or enlightened. That kind of new, manufactured self-image would only replace the old, deficient one. Selflessness and humility show up automatically when you see through the fundamental lie embedded in the words *There's something wrong with me.*

When you no longer believe in the core deficient self, you have less need to define yourself and others through mental stories, as if those stories actually were who you and others really are. You can meet others freshly in the moment, without the mental masks that keep you feeling separate. At that point, the heart can't help opening. You're no longer trying to protect yourself from feeling the painful emotions that accompany the core deficiency story. Psychological self-protection is necessary only if you take that story to be your real identity.

Seeing through the sense of deficiency does not mean negating your individual skills, talents, and other qualities. You retain your own unique expressions. Seeing through your core deficiency story simply means no longer experiencing yourself as separate and deficient. Who you are is no longer wrapped up in what you think about yourself. You can relax and simply be in the moment, without having to compare and contrast yourself with others. You no longer need to engage in fruitless seeking, or try to control others, or alienate yourself from others. When you see the core deficiency story as false, you find that you want everybody to succeed, and what arises in you is a deep care and compassion for everyone and everything.

Love, freedom, peace, balance, equality, and compassion characterize human experience in relationship when the beliefs in separation and deficiency are seen through. But don't take these words at face value, or merely as a new belief system. See for yourself. Let this reality become your direct experience. Do the inquiries.

CHAPTER 4

The Boomerang Inquiry

As you'll recall, the Unfindable Inquiry is the inquiry we use to see that a particular person, either self or other, is empty of separate nature. The Unfindable Inquiry focuses on one person at a time. The Boomerang Inquiry is what we call the Unfindable Inquiry when we use it on the core deficiency story as it shows up in relationship.

Like a boomerang that returns to the thrower, the deficient self is mirrored back to you in relationship. When you use the Boomerang Inquiry, you see that mirroring effect in action, and you also see through the deficient self that is being mirrored back to you. When you really believe that you're deficient at the core, almost anything can appear to confirm your deficiency story. As a result, you can use this tool to inquire into your relationship with a person, a place, an event, a goal, or anything else.

How the Boomerang Inquiry Works

1. **Look in the mirror.** Whenever you are triggered in relationship, find out what deficiency story some person or thing is mirroring back to you.

2. **Name the deficient self.** Give the deficient self a specific name, such as the "the unlovable self," "the one who is unfulfilled," "the lacking self," "the incomplete self," "the person who is broken," "the unsuccessful self," "the unsafe self," or "the invalid self."

3. **Find the deficient self.** Use the Unfindable Inquiry to try to find this deficient self.

You can see that the Boomerang Inquiry is very similar to the Unfindable Inquiry. It simply adds a new first step—using the mirror of relationship to find out what you believe about yourself. Just keep in mind that the Boomerang Inquiry applies whenever you are investigating how something outside yourself seems to bring up your sense of deficiency.

The Boomerang Inquiry: An Example

Tricia: Brian, my husband, triggers me almost every day. I catch him looking at other women. I notice that he doesn't listen to me, and this really bothers me. I've tried talking to him about emotions, but he can't talk about them. He says I'm overreacting to everything.

Scott: In those moments when you catch him looking at other women, how do you feel about yourself?

Tricia: Ugly. I feel like I'm not good enough for him.

Scott: How about the times when he isn't listening to you, or doesn't want to talk about the things you wish to talk about?

Tricia: I feel as if he's shutting me out, and that hurts.

Scott:	Now name the deficient self. If you could reduce this whole story about how he makes you feel to one specific kind of deficient self, what would it be? Reduce it down to something that really feels like you at the core.
Tricia:	I'm unlovable. That sums it up completely.
Scott:	Now find it. Try to find that unlovable self. Relax, and just notice the capacity to be aware of thoughts coming and going. Look right at the words "I'm unlovable." Are those words you—the unlovable self? If it helps, you can imagine putting those words inside a picture frame in your mind, to isolate them so you can look directly at them.
Tricia:	Let me take a moment.... Are the words "I'm unlovable" me? Yes, that's me. That's how I feel about myself.
Scott:	When words feel like who you are, it just means that some emotion or sensation is arising along with the words. But the emotion or sensation is unconscious. In other words, you aren't directly aware of it. Take a moment, bring attention into your body, and see what emotion or sensation is arising.
Tricia:	Sadness.
Scott:	Look right at the word "sadness." Frame it. Is that you—the unlovable self?
Tricia:	No, that's clearly just a word.
Scott:	Let that word fall away, and bring attention back into your body. Can you feel the energy that

you're calling sadness? Not the word "sadness," but the actual energy in your body?

Tricia: Yes.

Scott: Take a moment, and just notice that you're presently aware of that energy, without a name for it. Gently observe that energy. Is that energy you—the unlovable person?

Tricia: Yes, that's me.

Scott: Whenever an emotion or sensation feels like you, it just means there are some words or mental pictures arising along with it. If you just take a moment and look into your mind, what words or pictures are arising along with that energy?

Tricia: The words "I've always had this problem with men."

Scott: Look right at those words. Are those words you—the unlovable self?

Tricia: Those are just words. When I looked at them, they fell away.

Scott: Bring attention back into your body. Do you feel that energy still?

Tricia: Yes.

Scott: Look again at that energy, without labeling it. Just let all words and pictures relax. Observe. Is that energy you?

Tricia:	No, that's just energy. And it dissolved as soon as those words dissolved.
Scott:	Bring up a memory of the last time Brian wasn't listening to you, and you felt hurt.
Tricia:	That's not hard. He did it this morning.
Scott:	Look directly at that mental picture of you talking this morning, while he's not listening. Frame it, if that helps. Is that picture you?
Tricia:	No, that's just a memory. It's not me.
Scott:	Look at the words "He looks at other women." Are those words you—the unlovable person? Stick to yes or no. Don't elaborate.
Tricia:	No.
Scott:	How about "He doesn't listen to me, and this really bothers me"?
Tricia:	No.
Scott:	Just rest, and scan the space of your inner body. Let any word, picture, or energy arise naturally. Where is the unlovable person? Can you find her?
Tricia:	I don't know what you mean.
Scott:	You came to me saying that you're an unlovable person. I assume that this is who you've taken yourself to be for many years, right?
Tricia:	Yes, since childhood.

Scott:	If this is really who you are, shouldn't you be able to find that unlovable person right now? When a child is looking for an Easter egg, she isn't confused about what she's looking for. Either she spots it or she doesn't. If there's an unlovable person sitting with me here right now, can you point me to her?
Tricia:	Yes. It's me.
Scott:	Are the words "It's me" the unlovable self?
Tricia:	Ha-ha! No. Just words.
Scott:	Look for the unlovable person.
Tricia:	It seems to be in my name.
Scott:	Look directly and only at the word "Tricia." Is that the unlovable person?
Tricia:	No, but it seems to point to her.
Scott:	Find the unlovable person who's right here. Not just words pointing to her. Find *her*.
Tricia:	I can't. Wait…yes, I can. I see the thought *I know he loves me, but I don't feel it.*
Scott:	Are those words you, the unlovable person?
Tricia:	Well, intellectually, I know they're just words. But there's sadness arising again.
Scott:	Bring your attention into the body to feel that energy, without words or pictures. Is that energy you?

Tricia:	No. I can't find the unlovable me at all. I'm now just sitting here in peace, feeling totally free of that story. I can see the memory of my dad. He was cold. But when I look right at that picture, I can see it's not me, the unlovable person. Wait...there's a picture in my mind of me as a ten-year-old girl. That's the unlovable me.
Scott:	Is that picture of the girl you, the unlovable self?
Tricia:	I can see it's just a picture. I went straight into the body to feel the energy of sadness, and it washed through. No, it's not me. Wow, I've been in this story for a long time. I can't find her, the unlovable self.
Scott:	Take a look at Brian again in your mind. Does the sense that you're an unlovable person arise when you look at him? Is the boomerang at work again?
Tricia:	No, he looks perfect just as he is. I can see I love him. Actually, it's more than that. It's just love. I don't feel like it's missing. This was just a story I was placing on him. Thank you! Thank you! This is as clear as day now. I feel so much lighter!
Scott:	Yes, and when the story is *I'm unlovable*, we believe others contain our love, withholding it from us.
Tricia:	What a cruel joke!

Incorporating the Boomerang Inquiry into Your Life

Tricia sent out the message that she felt like an unloved person, and the message came back to her, like a boomerang. She followed her script and played the part, speaking the lines of an unloved person. She consistently reacted to Brian from that belief about herself, interpreting his actions as unloving. Whether Brian's actions were objectively unloving made no difference to Tricia's story. The interpretation was happening in Tricia's mind. The boomerang *I'm unloved* came right back to Tricia.

When we believe we're unlovable at the core, there's an unconscious drive within us to attract people and situations that confirm this deficiency story. We repeat the same pattern in our relationships. We continually interpret the actions of others according to that story. We may even unconsciously sabotage relationships. In these ways, over and over, we solidify the story until we finally see through the deficient self. Tricia was never a deficient person. There are no deficient people. There are just old scripts that go on running.

Notice that near the end of the inquiry, I asked Tricia to look again at Brian, after she discovered that she couldn't find the unlovable person. When she looked at him, she no longer felt that trigger. The deficient self was seen through. The old script *I'm an unlovable person* was no longer operating. Once we see that story to be unfindable, we see that love is our true nature. We naturally stop throwing the boomerang out, because the story of deficiency is absent. Others cannot return what we no longer throw out to them.

This doesn't mean that we have to stay in every relationship. Either we stay or we leave. The right action becomes clearer when we're no longer looking at others through the lens of a deficient self. For example, when someone's core story is *I'm unlovable*, she may unconsciously choose a partner who can't reciprocate love, who abuses her physically or emotionally, or who acts in other ways that appear unloving. Or she may unconsciously sabotage a healthy relationship in order to keep her core story of unlovability going. Although the result is pain, the pain is familiar. It reinforces her core identity. After all, who would she be without that core story? To make this point is not to blame the victim. And to say that she keeps her core story going is not to excuse any of her partner's abusive or problematic behavior. But this kind of insight can open her up to the possibility of seeing that her core story may have something to do with the people she chooses as partners, and with how she responds and reacts in relationships.

As she sees through her belief in her core deficiency, all that unconscious mental activity comes into the light of awareness and then quiets. The magnetic pull toward a partner who will mistreat her, a magnetic pull that has its basis in her own story of core deficiency, is finally released. Her sabotaging stops. She may decide to stay in the relationship if it deepens into a more mature, deficiency-free, selfless love. Or she may find that she's no longer interested in being with that particular partner, especially if her partner, unwilling to look within, is still acting out his or her own patterns of deficiency.

CHAPTER 5

The Panorama Inquiry

Recall what you learned in chapter 3 about the three steps involved in taking a panoramic view of your relationships with other people and things as a way of coming to see and name the core deficient self:

1. Imagine yourself sitting in the middle of a room, with all the other people and things in your life placed around you in a circle.

2. Scan around the whole circle.

3. As you look at each person or thing, notice how it appears to reflect back to you the idea that you are deficient in some way.

In a way, your life is already designed as a circle. All the people, situations, and events you encounter are all around you, feeding you information about who you are. Imagining this circle puts everything and everyone around you into focus. It allows you to see how each person and thing is mirroring back to you some version of the story *I am deficient*.

How the Panorama Inquiry Works

1. **Create a circle.** Imagine that your circle contains all the people and things in your life.

2. **Scan all around the circle.** Stop whenever you feel triggered in any way.

3. **Name the deficient self.** Give a specific name to the deficient self that a particular person or thing in the circle appears to have mirrored back to you.

4. **Find the deficient self.** Using the Unfindable Inquiry, try to find the deficient self you've named.

5. **Repeat.** Scan the circle again, repeating steps 2, 3, and 4 for each person or thing to whom or to which you react by feeling triggered.

As you move through this chapter and the chapters to come, notice that we're simply building on the Unfindable Inquiry. We're adding steps in order to illuminate the many ways in which the beliefs in separation and deficiency show up in different kinds of relationships.

The Panorama Inquiry is an extension of the Boomerang Inquiry. It just adds more people and things into the mix. The more people and things you add to your imaginary circle, the easier it is for you to see how the core deficiency story pervades all your relationships. And the more you see the core deficiency story operating in each of your relationships, the easier it becomes for you to use the Panorama Inquiry to see through that story.

No matter how you're triggered by the people or objects in the circle, you won't be able to find the deficient self. You'll see through all its manifestations. This inquiry ensures that no stone is left unturned.

The Panorama Inquiry: An Example

Kevin: I hate authority. I don't like it when people tell me what to do, or tell me what's best for me. I hate it when they pretend to know the truth about things. My mission is to show all authority figures how insane and arrogant they are.

Scott: Imagine yourself in the middle of a circle in which all the authority figures in your life are placed around you.

Kevin: I see my father, my high school principal, my boss, certain politicians, a spiritual teacher I followed around for a while, and my best friend, who's a know-it-all. And…let's see, who else? Oh yeah—you. I'm feeling that same resistance toward you because you believe you have this inquiry that's going to show me the truth.

Scott: [*laughing*] Sounds like you've attracted lots of authority figures!

Kevin: I don't attract them. They're just there. I just like to show them how arrogant they are.

Scott: Scan around the circle until you find yourself triggered, and then stop.

Kevin: I'm already triggered. My father stands out the most.

Scott: What deficient self does he mirror back to you? Name it.

Kevin:	I don't think I'm deficient. He just tried to control me, and he thought he knew what was best for me.
Scott:	How did it make you feel about yourself when he did that?
Kevin:	Small and weak.
Scott:	There's the deficient self.
Kevin:	Yikes. OK.
Scott:	Find it. See if you can find that person who's small and weak. Are the words "I feel small and weak" that person?
Kevin:	I'm feeling a real tightness in my chest.
Scott:	So that's a yes?
Kevin:	Yes!
Scott:	Are the words "I'm feeling a real tightness in my chest" that small and weak person?
Kevin:	No.
Scott:	Let those words fade away. Just notice them, and let them dissolve. Feel the energy in your chest without naming it. Just sit there for a while. Give yourself all the time you need. Let me know when you can feel just that energy, without naming it.
Kevin:	[silent for thirty seconds] Yeah, I feel it.
Scott:	Is that energy the small and weak person—the deficient you?

Kevin: No. It's fading.

Scott: Look at your father's face. Is that mental picture the small, weak person?

Kevin: No.

Scott: How about the words "He tried to control me"? Is that you?

Kevin: If I don't put the picture of his face with those words, and I just see the words, then…no. That's not me.

Scott: How about a memory of your father trying to control you, or telling you how to live your life? Can you see any memory of that? Is that memory you?

Kevin: Yes, that's me. The tightness is there again, along with fear.

Scott: Just sit and observe that picture, without interpreting it. Watch it fall away. Feel the energy in your body, without words and pictures. Is that energy you—the weak, small person?

Kevin: When I dropped that picture, the tightness left.

Scott: Take a moment and just relax, noticing your capacity to be aware. Look into your direct experience. Scan the inner space of your body. Look everywhere, just as a child does when he's looking for an Easter egg. The egg you're looking for is the small, weak person. Can you find it?

Kevin:	No, I can't find it. And right away I feel forgiveness for my father. I see that he had his own story.
Scott:	Create the circle again. Scan around it until you're triggered.
Kevin:	I see politicians. I see myself watching them on TV, and they're pretending to be the authorities for us all.
Scott:	Are the words "Politicians pretend to be the authorities for us all" you, the small, weak person?
Kevin:	No, those words aren't me. And that picture just fell away. Now I see my spiritual teacher. He acted like such a guru. He thought he had the truth. Anyone who disagreed with him was made to feel insignificant.
Scott:	So you felt insignificant?
Kevin:	Yes.
Scott:	See the pattern yet?
Kevin:	Yeah. "Insignificant" means small and weak.
Scott:	"He thought he had the truth." Are those words the small, weak you?
Kevin:	No. That's an idea. I know that. But I still feel that fear in my chest.
Scott:	Relax the idea, and feel the energy. Is that energy you?
Kevin:	Yes, this fear feels like me.

Scott:	Is the word "fear" you?
Kevin:	No. But that energy is me.
Scott:	That just means there are words or pictures still arising. What are they?
Kevin:	It's just a picture in my chest, like a black hole.
Scott:	Look directly at that image. Is that image you, the small and weak person?
Kevin:	Yes, that's me.
Scott:	Are the words "That's me" you, the small, weak person?
Kevin:	Interesting. No, I can see that's a thought. That's not me.
Scott:	When you aren't emphasizing the thought *That's me*, is that black hole a picture of you?
Kevin:	No. And now I see it loosening up.
Scott:	Just observe it gently, without describing what it means for you. Watch it morph and change on its own. What is it changing into?
Kevin:	A picture of a fist in my stomach, and a feeling of rage.
Scott:	Is that picture of the fist you, the small, weak person?
Kevin:	No. It's falling away. And now I just feel this boiling anger.
Scott:	Let it boil, but without words and pictures for it.

Kevin: I saw it rise up, as energy. And now it's releasing
           …into…peace.

Scott: Look back at your spiritual teacher. Are you
           triggered?

Kevin: Yes, but I'm looking at that thought. No, that's
           not me. That's not a weak, small person. It's just a
           picture of me, and the rest of his students sitting
           around him. There's no charge to it.

Scott: Scan the circle again.

Kevin: I'm seeing you there, and feeling a small charge.
           But in just feeling that feeling, it's releasing. I'm
           not seeing you as an authority figure. You're not
           telling me what's true. You're just helping me look
           at my own beliefs.

Scott: Scan the circle.

Kevin: I see my dad and my spiritual teacher, but they
           seem totally OK now. I feel no aggression toward
           them. But I see my best friend, Mark, who thinks
           he knows it all. I love the guy, but he pisses me off.

Scott: Are the words "He thinks he knows it all" you?

Kevin: No. And I can see that the words "He pisses me
           off" are not me, the small, weak person.

Scott: Can you find the small, weak person?

Kevin: No, it's nowhere to be found. Damn!

Scott: Scan around the circle. How does everyone else
           look now—all those authority figures?

Kevin:	I don't see anything wrong with them.
Scott:	Were you experiencing any peace by constantly trying to show these people the arrogance of their ways?
Kevin:	Not only was I not feeling peace, I wasn't changing them. They just continued saying and doing what they'd always said and done. And it just kept enraging me. So I fought and fought.
Scott:	But to no avail.
Kevin:	I might have changed one or two people slightly in my life by my constant raving against authority, but generally to no avail. Mostly a lot of damage done.
Scott:	Do you see how relationships harmonize when you stop focusing on others and just turn toward this deficient self and try to find it?
Kevin:	Yes. Oh my God, yes! I feel like I've been in a lifelong nightmare and I'm just waking up now.
Scott:	Scan the circle one more time. Are you triggered?
Kevin:	No, not at all.
Scott:	Just remember—whenever you're triggered, do this inquiry.
Kevin:	I will. I don't want to do this to myself anymore.
Scott:	It's great for you to see that you were doing this to yourself. When you clean up your mess, everyone else starts looking cleaner, too.

Kevin: Spotless! [*Laughs.*] There was only one spot—
         me—sitting there in the middle, making a mess
         of every relationship. But wait! Does this mean
         that all opinions are bad, and that I'm never
         supposed to speak my mind again? Is that what
         you're saying?

Scott: No. You can always speak your mind. We all
         learn from and influence each other in
         relationship. You'll probably find that your voice
         comes from a more authentic, honest place as you
         see that you're not a deficient person.

Kevin: Makes total sense. I can also see that there's not
         a lot to judge people about when I don't feel
         weak and small.

Incorporating the Panorama Inquiry into Your Life

The million-dollar question is this: Will you no longer be triggered in relationship after doing the Panorama Inquiry once?
The answer differs with each person.

In my work, I've noticed that some people see so clearly
through the deficiency story the first time they do the inquiry
that they never need to do it again. If they're triggered after doing
the inquiry, they immediately become aware of their thoughts,
emotions, and sensations, and they can allow them to come to
rest and don't have to go back into suffering.

For many others, the Panorama Inquiry becomes a tool that
they carry with them in their day-to-day lives. They use it every
time they're triggered, and they go through the whole set of questions. For some people, one result of the inquiry is that they begin

to see the deficiency story popping up everywhere and even, for a while, popping up more often. This is good news! It means that the story was always operating at some level, but that it was unconscious.

The Panorama Inquiry makes your core deficiency story more and more conscious. And the more you see your story, the more you free yourself from its grip. But you're not freeing yourself by force. As you use the Panorama Inquiry and also the Boomerang Inquiry, the core deficiency story begins to dissolve on its own, or it even stops arising. The story actually lets go of *you*, leaving you to rest naturally in the present moment.

I've noticed, however, that many people carry their deficiency stories into self-improvement work, into recovery, and into seeking something better or different. They look for a future in which they will have been cured of their core deficiency. But that future is actually mirroring back their sense of being currently deficient. In the same way, some people create a deficiency story around the inquiries.

For example, one woman did an inquiry and later told me that she'd realized her need to continue doing the inquiry in order to get rid of her deficient self somewhere down the road. She was using the inquiry as a way to keep believing that she was actually deficient. She thought there truly was something wrong with her, and that the inquiry would fix her. And so, in another session, instead of helping her buy into that belief about a deficient self that needed to be eliminated, I asked her to stop and try to find that deficient self. But she couldn't find it in that exploration. We both laughed as she noticed how she'd been using the inquiry to reinforce her belief in her core deficiency, and that belief was seen through on the spot.

Do you see how subtle the deficiency story can be? The fact is, there is no deficient self. There's only belief in the deficient self. If you believe that it's really here, and that you have to work toward getting rid of it in the future, then you're already buying into it as something real.

So here's a critical caveat: Be careful not to turn these inquiries into a new story about how you're a deficient person who needs to be fixed by the inquiries. They're not designed to help you seek some future moment in your story, a time when you'll finally be free. Thinking of the inquiries in that way just reinforces the notion that you're deficient now and will be fixed later on. The inquiries are designed for exploration in the present. Use them that way. And don't look at this book as a way of getting to some future point or state. Try, right now, to find the deficient self that believes freedom lies only in the future. If you can't find that self right now, then what is it that you're seeking from the future? Seeking a future state makes sense only if you currently buy into the idea of being a deficient self.

A Note on Using the Inquiries

This book contains a lot of information is intended to explain how the deficient self operates and to provide insight as you use the inquiries. But if this book just gives you more information about yourself, it won't necessarily transform you. So don't bog yourself down trying to memorize the words in these pages. Use the inquiries mainly when you're triggered in relationship. Spend most of the day just being aware of—present to—the thoughts, emotions, and sensations that come and go.

And remember that there can be a strong pull back into self-analysis as a way to keep the core deficiency story alive. If you're doing the inquiries but find yourself spinning into a bottomless pit of self-analysis, as I did when I couldn't distinguish the "branches" of my thoughts from the "trunk" of my deficiency story, take a break. The inquiries aren't meant to send you into even more mental activity focused on yourself. They're designed to reveal open, clear, spacious, thought-free, selfless rest as always and already present in your own direct experience. This is a quieting of the mind, not an activation of it. So take several days off, if you need to, and come back to the inquiries later.

In the meantime, stick with the simple approach described in the introduction to this book. Take brief moments of rest throughout the day, letting all words, pictures, and energies come and go freely within your experience.

CHAPTER 6

Conflict

For as long as there have been humans roaming the Earth, there has been conflict. Conflict arises out of the belief in separation—the notion that *I*, *you*, *we*, and *they* are all separate. There is conflict on all levels of human experience—between people, between groups, and between nations.

Conflict is not a dirty word. Conflict can be useful if you're willing to use it to go inward and see what it is that you believe about yourself. What's usually at the root of conflict is a belief about the self. Once that belief is explored, it can become a doorway to your deeper knowing that you are not a separate person.

If you look beyond the surface issue of who is right and who is wrong you will find that most conflict is about the fear of death. Being wrong is deeply threatening to the sense of *me*.

In the midst of conflict, if you pay close attention to the play of thoughts, emotions, and sensations, you will notice that it's the sense of self that is being protected and defended. Defending and protecting that sense of self, and attacking others who threaten it, can feel like a matter of instinctual survival—fight or flight. After all, when someone makes your *me* feel wrong, that person is not just threatening a random, uninteresting thought that you're having. If you believe that you *are* your thoughts and emotions, then it feels as if your very identity, your *me*, is being threatened.

Using the Boomerang Inquiry for Conflict

This chapter and others that follow contain examples of how I've worked with people by using the Unfindable Inquiry, the Boomerang Inquiry, and the Panorama Inquiry. As you become more familiar with each of these three inquiries, it will be easier for you to feel your way into which one works best in a particular situation. The following example involves Robert and his conflict with Charlie, a coworker. In this example, I helped Robert by using the Boomerang Inquiry.

Robert: I work with a guy named Charlie. We have lunch together. We always end up talking about politics, and the conversation always gets very heated. I want to be able to talk about politics without having our conversation turn into a fight.

Scott: Maybe the conversation isn't really just about politics.

Robert: I get what you mean. It gets very personal.

Scott: Let's use the Boomerang Inquiry. Use the mirror. When you look right now at Charlie, as Charlie tries to be right, what does that mirror show you about who you are?

Robert: I feel wrong.

Scott: Do you see how there's a sense of a separate, deficient person who has to defend and protect himself?

Robert: Yes. Like I said, it feels really personal.

Scott: Let's name it specifically. Let's just call it "the wrong self" or "the person who is wrong."

Robert: Yes, I've felt that many times throughout my life. This must be why I keep getting into these arguments. I want to be right.

Scott: Find it. When you look right now, can you find the person who is wrong? Are the words "I'm wrong" that person?

Robert: Something in my gut says yes, that's me.

Scott: Whenever words feel like *they* are who *you* are, it just means there's some sensation or emotion arising along with the words. What is that sensation in your gut?

Robert: A clenching sensation.

Scott: Are the words "clenching sensation" you, the wrong person?

Robert: No.

Scott: Just take a moment and let the words "I'm wrong" and "clenching sensation" come to rest. Rest here in the present moment, without your story, for a few seconds. Bring awareness to that energy in your gut. Is that energy you, the person who is wrong?

Robert: Yes, it feels like me.

Scott: Whenever an emotion or sensation in the body feels like who you really are, it just means some thought—some string of words, or a picture—is arising, too. Do you see anything like that? Look into your body. Is there a mental picture down there in your gut?

Robert:	I see a picture of my stomach.
Scott:	Is that picture you, the person who is wrong?
Robert:	No, it's just a picture.
Scott:	Just observe the picture, without placing any words on it. Watch it morph and change on its own.
Robert:	Yes, it's starting to disappear.
Scott:	Is there some emotion left over?
Robert:	Yes, fear, but it's starting to release now that the picture has disappeared. But it's not releasing totally.
Scott:	That's OK. Let it be as it is. The point of this is not to get rid of sensations or emotions. The point is to try to find the person who is wrong. I want you to pull up a recent memory of you and Charlie arguing over politics. What is he saying?
Robert:	That I'm confused, like all Democrats.
Scott:	You're "confused, like all Democrats." Are those words you?
Robert:	No, because I know that Democrats are not confused.
Scott:	This inquiry is not about politics. It's not even about what is true. It's about seeing if you can find the person who is wrong, that core deficient self that feels like it needs to defend and protect itself.

Robert:	OK, no. Those words aren't me. This is incredible. Something just fell away...a feeling of heaviness lifted. I was taking those words to be me. You're right—this isn't about politics. It's about me.
Scott:	Can you find the person who is wrong as you sit here resting, just letting thoughts arise and fall?
Robert:	Something is still hanging on. I'm seeing the thought *I need to show Charlie this inquiry.* That feels very personal, for some reason.
Scott:	Are the words "I need to show Charlie this inquiry" you, the person who is wrong?
Robert:	[*laughing*] No, that's not me. And I can see I just wanted to show him that he's wrong, and that this is not about politics at all.
Scott:	As you sit here, right now, can you find the person who is wrong?
Robert:	He's in my body.
Scott:	Are the words "he's in my body" you, the person who is wrong?
Robert:	No.
Scott:	Close your eyes, and scan the inner space of your body with awareness. Don't think. Just scan. Can you find the person who is wrong?
Robert:	No, I can't find him. But I sense that he is this body.

Scott:	Do you see the outline of your body when your eyes are closed?
Robert:	Yes.
Scott:	Can you see that it's a mental image or picture?
Robert:	Yes.
Scott:	Look at that line. Trace it all around the body, from head to toe. Is the mental image of a line you, the person who is wrong?
Robert:	When I look directly at that outline, I can see it's just a thought. I feel a great openness right now, like there's no line between me and the space around me.
Scott:	Look into that open space. Scan it. Can you find the person who is wrong?
Robert:	No.
Scott:	Now look back at Charlie's face. Are you triggered again?
Robert:	Not at all. I have no desire right now to argue with him. I couldn't care less.

Another Option

Instead of using the Boomerang Inquiry, I could have taken Robert through the Unfindable Inquiry and asked him to find Charlie as a separate, objective other. For example, I could have asked, "Is the picture of Charlie's face him? How about the words 'Democrats are confused'?" Sound is a sensation. I could have asked Robert to hear the sound of Charlie's voice. Then I could have asked, "Is that sound Charlie?" Questions like these could have helped reveal to Robert that when he was thinking, he was not experiencing a separate, objective Charlie. He was experiencing thoughts, emotions, and sensations that painted Charlie in a way unique to Robert. When that sense of separation is released, the need to be right is often released along with it.

More About Using the Inquiries for Conflict Situations

Sometimes in a debate, we believe we're using logic to try to come to the "objective" truth about a particular topic, but we're actually using logic as a way of reinforcing personal identity. A casual debate turns into a conflict when we believe that we're seeing things objectively, and we overlook the fact that what we're seeing is being filtered through our thoughts.

Thought is where personal identity resides. This is why debate often gets so personal. Emotions and sensations arise with thoughts and create a sense of personal identity that seeks above all else to be right. The more emotionally charged the viewpoint, the truer it can seem. In this way, the viewpoint isn't really based in logic. It's based in emotion. And when we're so completely identified with our thoughts that we mistake them for reality, being wrong can feel highly personal and threatening.

No viewpoint exists all by itself. A viewpoint cannot exist separately from other viewpoints, just as a person cannot exist separately from other people. Right cannot exist without wrong. The two arise together and are interdependent. That's why relationship functions as a mirror.

Does this seem like too much to take in? If so, try defending a viewpoint without having someone else to defend it against.

For conflict to occur, there must be two sides. One side cannot fight with itself. When you're defending a viewpoint for personal reasons, you're using that viewpoint as a way to define a self, a *me*, against an other. The more personally you identify with a viewpoint, the harder it is for you to hear someone else's perspective. You're so busy defending your own viewpoint that you stop listening.

When you find yourself in a heated debate, ask yourself whether you're defending the truth or defending a self. It's certainly healthy to be passionate about topics that you hold dear to your heart. And it's healthy to express how you think and feel about something that you're discussing with another person. There are situations in which you do have to stand up for what you believe is a more appropriate viewpoint. But you can do this without believing that your viewpoint has anything to do with a personal identity. You are not your thoughts. A thought is something that you experience. Thoughts come and go. Sometimes in discussions you may be deceiving yourself by thinking that you're just being passionate about a viewpoint when you're actually feeling personally threatened and are reacting from fear of being wrong.

When you're in a debate with someone else, how often do you use logic to support that person's view? Probably not very often. What's probably far more common is using logic to support your own view at the expense of the other person's perspective. And every time you make a point, that point becomes a way for you to solidify your image of the person who is making the point. Instead of finding the truth, you keep finding and reinforcing a self.

Instead of using conflict to solidify a self and reinforce the belief in separation, you can use conflict as a way to wake up out of that belief. You can see through the self that is identifying with thoughts—and the inquiries in this book can help. Once you're no longer using logic to reinforce the belief in separation, communication becomes more authentic. You're become more able to take in others' perspectives. And as all perspectives are taken into account, things no longer have to become deeply personal. In discussions with other people, you can still express your views freely, but you're liberated from the need to defend a self.

CHAPTER 7

Perfectionism

Perfectionism is the drive to change or perfect the self, others, and situations. There is often an underlying sense that things are not as they should be, and so improvement is constantly sought.

Not everyone has this tendency. But for those who do, an inner sense of inadequacy or imperfection is often projected or reflected onto other people or life circumstances. Perfectionists are not just hard on themselves—they frequently judge situations and other people as wrong or deficient in some way, too. This drive toward perfection can easily trigger a sense of deficiency in the ones being judged. As a result, many perfectionists report a recurrent pattern of frustration in their relationships.

The perfectionist's mind is trying to construct a perfect outer reality in order to fix an inner belief in deficiency. It's an exhausting effort, and it doesn't work. In this game, there are no winners. Even if the perfectionist succeeds at changing another person or a situation, there is always something else "out there" to be improved or changed. And the more perfectionists focus outward, the more blind they remain to the root of the issue, which is the belief *I am imperfect*. Outer circumstances are merely a reflection of this inner view of self.

Using the Boomerang Inquiry for Perfectionism

The key to using this inquiry is to turn toward the belief in an inadequate self and see that it is nothing but an empty fiction.

Zoe: I'm a perfectionist. I can't help it. I've always been that way. This is creating a lot of problems in my relationship. I'm always judging and trying to change my partner.

Scott: Does it feel like something is wrong with him, as if he shouldn't be the way he is?

Zoe: Yes. I just know he could be better. He's lazy.

Scott: When you look at your partner right now, in your mind, what does that bring up in you?

Zoe: I'm frustrated with him. I know that if he would change just a few things, life would be smoother for both of us. I'd stop nagging him.

Scott: I'd like you to stop focusing on your partner for a second, and focus on what his behavior mirrors back to you about whether you're deficient in some way. Name it.

Zoe: I judge myself even more harshly than I judge him.

Scott: Now we're getting somewhere. Just give a specific name to that self you're judging so we can look to see if that's who you really are.

Zoe: It's like…there's something wrong with me, too. That's been there all my life, the self-judgment.

OK, let me look and see if I can give a name to it.... Inadequacy.

Scott: Can you find that inadequate self in your experience right now? Are the words "I'm inadequate" you, the inadequate person?

Zoe: Yes. That's me.

Scott: When you're identifying with a thought, it means there's some emotion or sensation arising along with it. What is that emotion or sensation?

Zoe: Contraction. Frustration.

Scott: Is the word "contraction" you, the inadequate self?

Zoe: Yes, that's it.

Scott: Relax that word for a few seconds, and find out what it's like to be aware of that contracted sensation in your body, without calling it "contraction." Take your time. When you can feel it without a name, ask yourself, "Is this me, the inadequate person?"

Zoe: Yes, that's me.

Scott: Are there words still coming up with that energy?

Zoe: I don't see any words right now.

Scott: How about memories, mental pictures? Sometimes the picture can be so subtle that you don't see it until you really relax and just observe the inner space of your body. It can even be a picture of the body part that seems to contain that contracted energy.

Zoe: Yes. I can see a picture of my chest.

Scott: Is that picture you, the inadequate self?

Zoe: Yes. It almost feels like that area of my body is responsible for all the self-judging thoughts.

Scott: Just observe that picture, without any words. Scan the picture up and down, left and right. Are there any words on the picture?

Zoe: You mean written on the picture of my chest?

Scott: Yes.

Zoe: No. I see it's just a picture of a chest.

Scott: As crazy as this may sound, stop and listen to that picture. Quiet your mind long enough to notice whether the picture itself is speaking. Is it saying anything?

Zoe: No.

Scott: When you aren't interpreting it, is this picture the inadequate person?

Zoe: No. And I can see it changing now. But there is anger coming up. I'm angry at myself and my partner.

Scott: Are the words "I'm angry at myself and my partner" you, the inadequate self?

Zoe: No, that's not the inadequate me.

Scott:	So just let those words come to rest by observing them directly. Is the word "anger" you?
Zoe:	No, it's not me. But it feels really intense right now.
Scott:	Are the words "it feels really intense right now" you?
Zoe:	No.
Scott:	OK, let those words come to rest also. Really experience what anger is like when you aren't describing it or attributing it to someone. Just rest, and let that energy do whatever it wants to do. Treat it the way you treat the air around you. You can't make air go away, and you can't make it stay.
Zoe:	It's just energy. That's not me, either. Now it's losing intensity.
Scott:	Look for the inadequate self. Scan the space of your whole body with awareness. Be aware of the inside of every body part, your head, everything. Scan without thinking. Can you find that inadequate self?
Zoe:	No.
Scott:	OK, just let thoughts arise and fall. Can you find the inadequate person?
Zoe:	I see the thought *I'm not doing this right*. I can see that I'm trying to do this inquiry perfectly, too.
Scott:	Are the words "I'm not doing this right" you?

Zoe:	No. Now I can't find me, the inadequate person. It's just not here now.
Scott:	Now look back at your partner. Does he seem to trigger that sense of inner inadequacy in you?
Zoe:	Yes. I feel like I'm wrong for judging him all the time.
Scott:	Are those words you?
Zoe:	No. Something just dropped away. He isn't triggering anything now when I think about him.
Scott:	Can you find the inadequate person as you sit here right now?
Zoe:	No. And so I can see there's nothing wrong with him or me.
Scott:	So what's not perfect about you or him?
Zoe:	There's nothing that needs to be changed.
Scott:	Right. Once you see that you can't find the inadequate person you take yourself to be, suddenly others don't look inadequate, either.
Zoe:	It's that simple?
Scott:	Yes. It only becomes complicated when you're focusing just on him, analyzing his behavior. In those moments, you're believing your thoughts about him instead of trying to find yourself. The inadequate self is like a layer of film on your eyeball. It distorts everything you see. That's why you've been so busy trying to change people and

situations around you. When you look for that inadequate self, you're turning your attention toward that layer of film. It's just an old script that says, "There's something wrong with me." It's not who you really are. It never was. There was never anything wrong with you. When you can't find that self, the layer begins to dissolve. You see other people the way they really are. There's nothing wrong with them, either.

Zoe: Magnificent. Such clarity now!

More About Perfectionism

Zoe is only one of many self-confessed perfectionists I've worked with over the years, people who have reported back to me that this inquiry helped them. But the natural relaxation of perfectionist tendencies doesn't keep people from using discrimination in their lives. In fact, many perfectionists have told me that after doing this inquiry, they became able to make more loving and compassionate use of their capacity to discriminate. Once they were freed from the basic belief *There's something wrong with me*, their discriminating minds turned away from negative judgments of self and others, and toward a natural creativity that saw everything as already perfect, just as it was.

And yet the movement to create change can still arise. The difference is that when perfectionists see through the sense of an inherently imperfect self, there is naturally less stress and frustration behind the viewpoints that arise to create change, and it becomes possible to see a natural perfection everywhere because the movement to create change no longer comes from the underlying belief in deficiency. Circumstances can be improved, without a corresponding belief that things are wrong.

There's no substitute for the lived experience of this gorgeous paradox. When creativity is freed from the imprisoning belief that things are wrong, it flourishes, and discrimination becomes naturally more selfless in nature. People who do this inquiry often tell me that their relationships have become more harmonious, too, and that others around them feel less judged. In addition, people who do this inquiry have reported feeling more freedom to act decisively, and even to act with what might look like tough love when the situation warrants it.

CHAPTER 8

Ambition

Ambition is the desire for success—for personal advancement, power, control, fame, or money. It may outweigh concern about how our actions affect others. It is often based in fear and in a core deficiency story, such as *I'm lacking* or *I'm incomplete.*

Aspiring to act in the world in a manner that truly cares for self, others, and all of life is not destructively ambitious. That kind of aspiration doesn't come from a core deficient self. It's more selfless and expansive in nature.

Discerning the difference between self-centered ambition and selfless action can be tricky. We may think we're being self-less when in fact we're welcoming suffering into our relationships with others. As long as we're operating from a personal sense of lack or incompleteness, we're often blind to the motivations that drive us.

Using the Panorama Inquiry for Ambition

John: My company has made a major profit this year
          through software development. Yet I feel this
          sense that we need to do more. Our competitors
          are catching up with us. The consumer base for

our products is limited. Our software helps people, so I don't think we're overly ambitious.

Scott: Then why did you come here to do this inquiry?

John: Well, there's a nagging feeling in my gut that something is off when I think about our company, the competitors, the consumers, and all the material items I own. I can't put my finger on it. I'm hoping you can help.

Scott: Imagine yourself in the middle of a circle. Place all the people and things in your company around you, along with your company's competitors and the potential consumers of your company's products. Scan the circle, and tell me if that nagging feeling shows up in your gut.

John: You threw me for a loop there. I thought you were going to have my company be in the middle of the circle, not me.

Scott: Companies aren't ambitious. People are. A company is just a group of people. And since we don't have the other people in your company here, or your company's competitors and the potential consumers of the company's products, we can just put you in the middle.

John: When I scan the circle and see potential consumers, I can see that whether they buy our products or not matters a great deal to me.

Scott: Don't forget to put the consumers who refuse to buy your company's products in the circle, too. What do they mirror back?

John:	Fear. I'm afraid many people won't buy the products.
Scott:	Name it. Name the deficient self. What's that feeling saying about you, the person?
John:	Lack. It's a fear of lacking money and security.
Scott:	Can you find the lacking self? Are the words "I'm afraid many people won't buy the products" you, the lacking self? Stick to yes or no.
John:	Yes.
Scott:	Let those words dissolve, and bring your naked observation to that feeling. Is that energy you?
John:	Yes, it feels like it.
Scott:	That just means there are still words or pictures arising. What are they?
John:	I'm going to lose everything I own.
Scott:	Are those words you, the lacking person?
John:	Yes.
Scott:	Do you see how thoughts, emotions, and sensations seem welded together, how they make you feel as if there's a person here who's lacking at the core?
John:	Yes.
Scott:	Whenever thoughts and emotions seem welded together, go back and forth between them. Bring your attention to the words, and then to the

energy without the words, and then back to the words, and then back to the energy without the words—back and forth. Do you see that the words have a quality different from the quality of the energy?

John: Yes, the words are just words. Those aren't me. But the energy feels more real. There's something about this fear in my body that feels like me.

Scott: Look directly at the energy, without the words, now that you know those words aren't you. Is this energy you, the person that lacks?

John: No, that's just energy. I see that now. Without a story, it doesn't have much force to it.

Scott: Look back at those consumers who won't buy the products. Is that mental picture of them you, the lacking self?

John: No.

Scott: Relax without thoughts for just a few seconds. Just notice your capacity to be aware. Scan everywhere in that awareness. Can you find the lacking person?

John: No, it's not there. So I'll scan the circle again. I can see the boss of my company pop up in the circle. I'm feeling the sense that something is off again. He could fire me at any moment.

Scott: Are the words "something is off" the lacking person?

John:	No, they're just words. And now I'm looking at the words "he could fire me at any moment." Those are not me, either.
Scott:	But does it feel like there's still a lacking self sitting right here with me?
John:	Not right now.
Scott:	Scan the circle, and see if you get triggered again.
John:	Yes. I see a memory of watching our competitors come out with some software that became popular.
Scott:	Is that mental picture the lacking self? It might help to put it into a frame in your mind. Make a mental image of a picture frame, and then put that memory inside the frame.
John:	Yes, that feels like me, for some reason, even though I'm nowhere in the picture.
Scott:	Relax those words. Feel the bodily energy that came up. Is that you?
John:	The energy relaxed. No, it's not me. OK, now I see my father, when I was young, sitting at the dinner table and worrying about money.
Scott:	Is that mental picture you, the lacking self?
John:	Yes, that's me… I'm resting into the energy without those words now… OK, no, the energy isn't me. A peace just fell over me. I don't have that feeling that something is off anymore. And I can't find the person who's lacking. I can see that

I've been deceiving myself. I've been telling myself that I'm just doing this job to pay the bills, and that's my only motivation. But I can see now that this story of lack has been completely running the show.

Scott: Paying your bills is good.

John: Yes, of course. And my bills have been paid. Actually, I've made a lot of money. But now I can see the real motivation for what I'm doing. I'm motivated by this core belief that I'm lacking. And I can't find that belief now. So my motivation is gone. That scares me. Does this mean I won't care about working for the company anymore?

Scott: It doesn't necessarily mean that. It means that you no longer have to be fueled by something that's not really there—a self that seems to lack something at the core.

John: Now I'm thinking about my future. I feel a striving to achieve.

Scott: That's great.

John: I've had lots of fun at my job and felt really inspired. But as I look at the future, it doesn't feel like inspiration. More like fear.

Scott: Put your future in the circle. Better yet, put a future there in which you aren't able to achieve what you want. Is the mental picture of that future you, the lacking person?

John: I see right away that there's nothing but words. And the fear was coming from believing those words. Yes, that feels good. I can relax a lot more in my life and tend to other things that I enjoy, and to my family, friends, and hobbies. And I can still work at my company, but without this story. I've been taking this job home with me every day. And it seems like everything has been about this fear and this lack.

Scott: Maybe you've taken the story *I lack* home with you every day because you thought it was you.

John: Right. Of course. Yes! The job is still there. It's the sense of lack that I can't find now. My job looks totally different, and so do all the people in the circle. I can see that they're all thoughts. I can see that I also took thoughts to be myself. So there's much less stress right now. My mind is much quieter around all this stuff.

More About Ambition

After doing this inquiry, John reported back to me that he continued to experience freedom from self-centered ambition. He was able to take the inquiry into his job on a daily basis. He continues to experience relaxation from the story *I lack*.

I've seen a variety of results from using this inquiry for ambition with many other people over the years. For example, there can be a kind of downtime before someone's true purpose reveals itself. Some people feel a bit directionless for a while, after realizing that much of what they've been doing in their careers has come from a basic sense of lack. As that sense of lack relaxes, these people's desire to continue working in their particular fields falls away.

Other people immediately discover new careers for themselves. They become very clear about what matters most to them. One woman in particular jumped wholeheartedly into a new business after doing this inquiry. For years she'd been driven by a sense of lack, but her newfound clarity allowed her to do what she really wanted to do, without the self-pressure she'd been feeling for so many years.

Doing this inquiry changed my own desire to be an attorney. I found that what had been driving me—the sense of lack—was no longer there. This discovery led me into being of service to others by using these inquiries in private sessions and in groups. For me, ambition based in lack has sneaked back in now and again, but that lack has been seen through with the use of this inquiry, and I've become very clear that nothing is lacking in myself or others. That realization brings deep relaxation into all my efforts to help people. When we're no longer operating from the story *I lack*, there's is a natural flow to life that can be trusted completely.

CHAPTER 9

Bullying

Both bullying and being bullied create and reinforce core deficiency stories. (In this book, the word "bullying" means improper treatment of someone within a non-familial social relationship, not improper treatment of someone within a marital or familial relationship.) Bullying, which often starts when people are very young, comes out of low self-esteem and feelings of powerlessness and inadequacy. When we don't see through the stories of deficiency as we're growing up, bullying can continue into adulthood. It happens in work relationships, on the Internet, and in just about every other situation imaginable. The Boomerang Inquiry and the Panorama Inquiry can be used by those who are bullying as well as by those who are being bullied.

Using the Boomerang Inquiry for Being Bullied

In this example, Werner was inquiring into feelings of not being good enough, feelings that were the result of his being bullied in his workplace.

Werner: I'm being bullied at work almost every day. It's gotten to the point where I just want to quit. I can't take it anymore. I've actually fantasized about being violent one day—walking into work and putting them all in their place.

Scott: Are your employers able to do anything about it?

Werner: My immediate boss bullies me, too, along with my coworkers. They all talk about me behind my back, and they call me names to my face—like "Werner the slow learner," because I ask a lot of questions during group meetings.

Scott: Create a circle in which you're sitting in the middle and surrounded by everyone at work who's bullying you. Use the mirror. When you look at all these people, how do you feel about yourself?

Werner: I start believing the names they call me.

Scott: Can you tell me a couple of the other names?

Werner: The worst one is "assface," because I'm ugly.

Scott: I see that this is what they call you. How do you see yourself? Name it. When you hear those thoughts in your head, what do they tell you about who you think you really are?

Werner: A loser who's not good enough.

Scott: I know that's what your thoughts tell you, but if you're really a loser who isn't good enough, then we ought to be able to find him, right?

Werner: Yes.

Scott: Let's try to find you.

Werner: OK...

Scott: I want you to relax in your chair and get really comfortable. Take a few deep breaths. Then I want you to notice that there are thoughts coming and going in your head.

Werner: I notice them.

Scott: I want you to pull up the words "a loser who isn't good enough" and just stare right at them, without adding any other words to them. Imagine those words in a picture frame in your mind, if it helps. Are those words you?

Werner: Definitely.

Scott: How do you feel in your body when you believe that those words are you?

Werner: Really sad.

Scott: OK. I want you to imagine the words "I'm really sad" in a picture frame in your mind. Are those words you, the loser who isn't good enough?

Werner: Yes, all these words feel like me. They're too close, you know? I can't see them as only words.

Scott: OK. Take this paper and this pen, and write down the words "I'm a loser who isn't good enough."

Werner: [*writing down the words*] OK.

Scott: Now look directly at those words on the page. Are those words you?

Werner: I get some distance from them now, seeing them on paper. But I still have to say yes because there's sadness welling up as I read them.

Scott: Can you feel that energy in your body? Don't think about it. Just feel it.

Werner: Yes.

Scott: Is that energy you, the loser who isn't good enough?

Werner: It's just an uncomfortable feeling.

Scott: Write down the words "it's just an uncomfortable feeling." Are the words on that page you, the loser who isn't good enough?

Werner: Looking at the words on the page, I'd have to say no.

Scott: OK. Now bring a very light quality of attention to the feeling itself, without adding any words to it. Take your time. Relax as awareness. Is that feeling, by itself, the loser who isn't good enough?

Werner: Yes, that feels like me.

Scott: Write down the words "yes, that feels like me." Are those words you?

Werner: No.

Scott: Now experience that feeling again, without even placing those words on it. Is that feeling you? Don't try to push the feeling away—just bring a light attention to it. Look at the feeling directly, without any ideas about it.

Werner:	No, that's not me, the loser.
Scott:	Now I want you to bring up a mental picture, a memory, of when you were bullied at work recently. Do you see that?
Werner:	Yes.
Scott:	Relax, and look directly at that picture. Is that you? It's yes if your body reacts in any way. It's no if your body doesn't react.
Werner:	Yes—immediate anger.
Scott:	Write down the words "immediate anger." Are those words you, the loser who isn't good enough?
Werner:	[*pausing in silence*] No...ha-ha! It's just energy, and it feels kind of pleasant when I just let it be there as it is.
Scott:	Now look back at the picture of being bullied at work. Is that picture you?
Werner:	I don't know. There's still a charge to it.
Scott:	OK. So remember, if there's any charge, just say yes.
Werner:	Yes.
Scott:	When words or pictures feel like you, the loser who isn't good enough, it means the words or pictures feel welded together with emotions or sensations. That's the Velcro effect. Do you know what Velcro is?

Werner:	Yes. I have Velcro on my weight bench at home. I use it to keep my hands fastened to the barbell. Yes, I can see the Velcro effect between my thoughts and the emotions.
Scott:	That Velcro effect is how self-identification happens. See that?
Werner:	Yes.
Scott:	Does it seem like the mental picture of being bullied is stuck to the feeling of anger?
Werner:	Yes.
Scott:	Sometimes when the Velcro effect is happening, there's a subtle mental picture of a body part, or some shape or form around the emotion. Relax, and bring gentle attention to the feeling. Do you see any picture like that?
Werner:	Yes. It's a bunch of steel bars over the feeling.
Scott:	Relax, and look directly at that mental photograph of steel bars. Is that picture you, the loser who isn't good enough?
Werner:	No. It's fading. But now I see a picture of a little boy being teased at school. That's me.
Scott:	Look directly at that picture. Is that you, the loser who isn't good enough?
Werner:	Hmmm…I don't know…no, now that I look again, that little boy is fading, too. But the words "you suck at everything" are coming up.

Scott:	Look right at the words. Are those words, by themselves, the loser who isn't good enough?
Werner:	No, those are just words. When I looked directly at them, without adding more words, they faded, and the charge in my body faded.
Scott:	How about the word "assface"?
Werner:	That seems like me. I can feel the sadness again.
Scott:	Sit there, allowing the energy to be, without trying to understand it or label it. Then ask yourself if that energy is you, the ugly loser. Take your time.
Werner:	No, it's just energy. It's so healing to just let these feelings flow naturally!
Scott:	Look back at the word "assface." Is that word, by itself, the loser who isn't good enough?
Werner:	By itself? No. Wow, this is interesting. I'm seeing all this dissolve in front of me.
Scott:	How about the words "Werner the slow learner"?
Werner:	No, those words aren't me. They look like silly rhyming words. It's kind of funny now.
Scott:	As you relax as awareness, can you find the loser who isn't good enough?
Werner:	[laughing] No, I feel an incredible weight off my shoulders right now. I feel free. But... somehow it feels like the loser is still here, waiting in the wings.

Scott: Look at the words "the loser is still here, waiting in the wings." Are those words, by themselves, the loser?

Werner: No.

Scott: Do you see any picture of a loser waiting in the wings somewhere?

Werner: Yes. I see a picture of him peeking around the corner, waiting for you to finish with me so he can come back out.

Scott: Look at those words. Are those words you, the loser who isn't good enough?

Werner: No, the words are not the loser.

Scott: Look at the picture of that figure peeking around the corner. But look without any words. Is that picture you, the loser who isn't good enough?

Werner: No. It's fading now...

Scott: Look at a future picture of you walking into work and being violent toward all those people. Is that picture you? Relax, and just look directly at the picture. Take all the time you need.

Werner: Ha—no. That's not even interesting now. That's not the loser.

Scott: Sit there, resting while being aware, letting everything be as it is. Whether there's thinking or no thinking, feeling or no feeling, can you find the loser who isn't good enough?

Werner:	[*smiling*] No! It's amazing how long this story has been there. I've totally believed it.
Scott:	Scan the circle of bullies now. Does the sense of being a loser who isn't good enough arise within you?
Werner:	No. In fact, they just look like middle-aged men.
Scott:	Do you see how going to the root and looking for the deficient self is how the most direct freedom is found?
Werner:	Absolutely!
Scott:	We continue to think of ourselves as deficient only because we don't look. We *think about* ourselves instead of *looking for* that self.
Werner:	Yes, that's so obvious right now. I was focusing so much on them that I wasn't seeing what I believed about myself. From now on, I'm going to look for that self instead of just buying into this story.

Bullies Feel Deficient, Too

Werner was the target of bullying, and so the inquiry centered on the belief in core deficiency that was showing up for him. But what if we'd been able to do the inquiry with the coworkers who were bullying him? We would have seen deficiency stories operating there, too. Bullies are often overcompensating for a deep sense of deficiency in themselves, a sense accompanied by feelings of inadequacy, insecurity, or weakness. They deflect that deficiency and project it onto others. It's safer for them to target that deficiency as something "out there," outside themselves. That story of core deficiency constitutes a blind spot. The story itself is difficult to see, and it's even more difficult to face once it is seen.

Regardless of whether one is bullying or being bullied, it's a matter first of naming the deficiency that's running the show and then actually trying to find it. In Werner's case, this didn't mean that he had to continue working at his current job. He might have found clarity about the whole situation and then discovered that he didn't want to work in that atmosphere anymore. Or he might have stayed and continued to see through all the projections coming from others. Either way, the inquiries would have given him deep insight into how deficiency gets tied into identity, and into the fact that the words "I'm a loser who isn't good enough" were not really who he was.

More About Using the Inquiries

Are you using these inquiries as a way of seeking the future or overintellectualizing yourself or others? An overactive mind or a restless energy in your body is a good indication that you're using the inquiries to seek the future or overintellectualize. Spend the majority of your day just resting, letting all words, pictures, and bodily energies be as they are. Notice that when you rest that way, there's nothing you have to do with or about thoughts, emotions, and sensations. They enter and leave awareness, leaving no trace. Use these inquiries only when you're triggered in relationship.

CHAPTER 10

Abuse

Through the years, I've worked with those who have abused others and with those who have been abused. Abuse comes in so many forms that it's hard to find one definition that truly fits all cases. But I define abuse—whether physical, sexual, emotional, or verbal—as improper, often violent, treatment of an individual or a group. (In this book, the word "abuse" means improper treatment of someone within a marital or familial relationship, whereas the word "bullying," as we saw in chapter 9, means improper treatment of someone within a non-familial social relationship.)

Deficiency stories permeate abusive relationships, on both sides of the equation. The first inquiry in this chapter was with Juliette, a woman who reached out to me because of ongoing verbal abuse from her husband. The second inquiry was with Zan, a thirty-five-year-old man who brought up something that had begun to rule his life—a desire to molest children.

Using the Boomerang Inquiry for Being Abused

Juliette: I've been married for fifteen years to a man who abuses me, verbally and emotionally. He yells and calls me names. Sometimes I think I even deserve some of the abuse he gives me. I'm too afraid to speak up. When I do speak up, he uses that against me.

Scott: When you look at your husband's face right now, as a mental picture, what does he mirror back to you about being deficient in some way?

Juliette: That I'm completely invalid.

Scott: Can you find that invalid self as you sit here talking to me?

Juliette: Well, I know that all of these are just thoughts, and that thoughts are not what I am.

Scott: You may know that intellectually, perhaps because you've read spiritual teachings that say, "You are not your thoughts," but does it feel like you're really an invalid woman?

Juliette: Yes, it feels like more than thoughts. I am invalid.

Scott: Look directly at the words "I am invalid." Are those words you, the invalid woman?

Juliette: Yes.

Scott: This means that some emotion or sensation is arising with the words. What is arising?

Juliette: Fear...and sadness.

Scott: Let's start with the fear. Is the word "fear" you, the invalid woman?

THE UNFINDABLE INQUIRY

Juliette: That word is not me, but I am afraid.

Scott: Let the word "fear" come to rest for a few seconds. Just look at it directly until it dissolves. That word is not the fear itself. It's a word pointing to energy in the body. Can you feel the actual energy in your body, when you aren't labeling it?

Juliette: Yes.

Scott: I want you to rest into that feeling, without adding any words or pictures to it. Rest, and allow the feeling to be there as it is, without trying to make it go away or labeling it. I'll drop out for a while as you do that.

Juliette: I can't be with the fear. I keep seeing his face, and memories of things he's said to me.

Scott: Are the words "I can't be with the fear" you, the invalid woman?

Juliette: No.

Scott: How about the words "I keep seeing his face, and memories of things he's said to me"?

Juliette: No, those words aren't the invalid me.

Scott: Look at the picture of his face in your mind. Is that picture you, the invalid woman?

Juliette: No, that's just a picture of him.

Scott: Look at the most prominent memory in your thought stream, a memory where he's said something that frightened you.

Juliette:	I hear him yelling at me, telling me that nobody will love me if I leave him.
Scott:	Look at the words "nobody will love me if I leave him." Are those words you, the invalid woman?
Juliette:	They feel true.
Scott:	OK, but I'm not asking if they feel true. I'm asking if those words are the invalid woman. Remember, we're trying to find that invalid woman.
Juliette:	Those words are not me.
Scott:	Can you find the invalid woman the words seem to point to?
Juliette:	I feel the fear in my chest again. I'm afraid of him.
Scott:	Are the words "I feel the fear in my chest again" the invalid woman?
Juliette:	No.
Scott:	How about the words "I'm afraid of him"?
Juliette:	Yes, that feels like me.
Scott:	That means there's an emotion or a sensation arising along with the words. I presume it's fear. Can you sit now and allow the energy of fear to be as it is, without words and pictures?
Juliette:	Yes.
Scott:	Is that energy itself the invalid woman?

Juliette:	[*long pause*] No, it's just energy. And when I'm not feeding it with stories, it loses its strength. That's nice…
Scott:	Look again at the words "I am invalid." Picture them in a frame. Are those words you, the actual invalid woman?
Juliette:	No, now they just look like words.
Scott:	Can you find the invalid woman?
Juliette:	I feel an incredible sadness, as if I've wasted many years of my life with a man who doesn't respect me.
Scott:	Look at the words "I feel an incredible sadness." Are those words you?
Juliette:	No.
Scott:	How about "I've wasted many years of my life with a man who doesn't respect me"? Imagine there's a typewriter in your head spelling out those words. Look at all the letters, one at a time. Are those words you?
Juliette:	Yes. I mean…I can see that they're words, but they feel like me.
Scott:	Is there sadness arising along with the words?
Juliette:	Yes.
Scott:	The words and the emotion can feel as if they're welded together, until you observe the emotion without adding words to it. Then you can see that

the emotion isn't really welded to the words. It's just energy that needs to arise and pass through. Can you rest and just let that energy be as it is, without words and pictures?

Juliette: Yes. And now those words are gone. The feeling, once I let it be there, turns to warmth. I feel present.

Scott: Can you find the invalid woman?

Juliette: No. I just feel spacious, warm, like a loving energy everywhere.

Scott: Look back at your husband's face. Does that seem to bring up the sense that you're an invalid woman?

Juliette: Yes, but it's much more subtle now. There aren't any words or pictures. Just a sense that I'm invalid.

Scott: Are the words "just a sense that I'm invalid" you, the invalid woman?

Juliette: No.

Scott: Can you find that sense when you aren't labeling it? Where is it?

Juliette: In my stomach—a tightness.

Scott: Are those words you?

Juliette: No.

Scott: Where is the invalid woman?

Juliette: It's this body. This body is invalid.

Scott: Are the words "This body is invalid" you, the invalid woman?

Juliette: [*giggling*] No. It's funny how words sneak in there to make me believe that. No, those words are not me. But it's the body itself that feels invalid, not the words.

Scott: With your eyes closed, I want you to bring the outline of your body into focus. Trace that outline from the top of the head down your side, to your feet, and back up the other side, until you reach the top of your head again. Do you see the line that seems to contain you, an invalid woman?

Juliette: Yes—that's what I'm saying. The body seems to contain me, someone who has no worth or validity.

Scott: Is that line, by itself, you, the invalid woman?

Juliette: No, not at all. I see that it's an image.

Scott: Where is the invalid woman?

Juliette: I have a sense that it's inside this image.

Scott: Are the words "I have a sense that it's inside this image" you, the invalid woman?

Juliette: No, those words are not me.

Scott: Without thoughts, scan the inside of that image. Scan that space left and right, up and down. Can you find the invalid woman?

Juliette:	I can't find the invalid woman at all. It's a total fiction that I've believed for years. I feel incredibly light and spacious, as if there's no invalid woman here at all. I don't feel any boundaries around me. In some way, this spaciousness feels like I'm life itself, which is totally valid. But my eyes are closed. I feel that if I open my eyes, the invalid woman will be here.
Scott:	Then open your eyes. Can you find the invalid woman with your eyes open?
Juliette:	I see my body. And somehow that looks like an invalid woman.
Scott:	Are the words "I see my body" the invalid woman?
Juliette:	[giggling again] No!
Scott:	How about the words "somehow that looks like an invalid woman"?
Juliette:	No—just words.
Scott:	Touch your leg. Is that sensation, by itself, the invalid woman? Don't place any words or pictures on the sensation. Just experience the sensation of touch by itself.
Juliette:	No, that sensation is not an invalid woman. And now, as I touch other parts of my body, those sensations are not it, either.
Scott:	Are any of the colors or shapes of your body an invalid woman?
Juliette:	[laughing] No—just colors.

Scott:	Close your eyes. Can you find the invalid woman?
Juliette:	No.
Scott:	Now open your eyes. Can you find the invalid woman?
Juliette:	No. What a relief this is! What incredible relief. The whole weight of that story is gone.
Scott:	Look back at your husband's face. Does the invalid woman show up again?
Juliette:	No. He just looks like a middle-aged man. He looks sad. I can see that he has believed things about himself. He doesn't know this love that I'm experiencing now. He must be really hurting inside to want to hurt me.
Scott:	How does the relationship feel, now that you're clear about not being an invalid woman?
Juliette:	Well, without this fear, I feel empowered to leave. I mean, I would love for him to change. But I don't see it happening. I can see how this fear has kept me trapped.
Scott:	Right! Seeing through the story of deficiency can bring utter clarity about what you want to do, whether that's staying or leaving. It clears the mind and opens the heart. Seeing through that story doesn't mean you have to stay and take whatever he dishes out. You don't have to be a doormat. But of course I can't give you advice about what to do. With this newfound clarity, you are the authority for your own life now.

Juliette:　Yes, and it's not that I'm telling the story that I'm a valid person now. Somehow it's a validity beyond the mind. It seems very clear that I want to leave this relationship. And now I think I can do it.

More About Being Abused

Juliette met with me several times after this inquiry. Occasionally she fell back into believing that there was something wrong with her, or that she was invalid and paralyzed by fear. Each time we met, I took her through the inquiry. Eventually she was able to do the inquiry on her own. She is now in the process of getting a divorce and moving on with her life. Juliette is a success story.

A few of the people I've met with over the years did not follow through with the inquiry and instead fell back into a sense of being stuck in the deficiency story. For example, I met with a woman who used the inquiry to find freedom from the story *I'm a lonely person*, only to fall back into that story. She didn't contact me for a whole year. After the year had passed, she set up another session and told me that she had been somewhat depressed. She had forgotten the freedom she'd experienced through the inquiry. We did the inquiry again, and she walked away free and clear of that story. She hadn't been quite ready the first time we met. There is nothing I can do for someone who is unwilling or unable to be with the painful emotions that lie at the heart of these stories. There is often a magnetic pull toward thinking of oneself as broken at the core.

The power that Juliette experienced came from the recognition that she herself was not a story. She didn't end up with the story *I am a valid person.* She recognized a profound presence. Notice that she called it "a validity beyond the mind." She was experiencing a non-dual recognition—she realized that she was beyond both deficiency and non-deficiency. The inquiries in this book open you to a knowing of clear, open, spacelike Oneness. In that openness, you begin to see everyone and everything as perfect, valid, and loving.

If you find yourself feeling trapped in an abusive relationship, seek help. You may benefit from therapy or some other program or method. The inquiries in this book are not therapy in the traditional sense of the word. In many (not all) forms of therapy, the focus is on replacing an old deficiency story with a new story, such as *I am a valid person*. If that's what you're looking for, then you may benefit more from therapy than from these inquiries. They're not designed to provide a better story, although you may choose to mentally land on a new one, and they're not about improving your personal story and defining yourself as better or more valid than others. Instead, the inquiries are designed to free you from *all* stories. In any case, whether you believe you'll benefit more from these inquiries or from traditional therapy, find and use whatever works for you.

Using the Panorama Inquiry for Being an Abuser

My work with people who abuse others sexually, physically, verbally, or emotionally has shown me that they suffer from deficiency stories, just as the victims of abuse (and so many other people) do. This doesn't in any way excuse their behavior. But working with the inquiries to heal the sense of deficiency in an abuser or potential abuser can help free them from wanting to act out against others.

As long as they're pointing outward and focusing on others, those who are prone to abusive impulses are unlikely to look within themselves. Conversely, when abusers, or potential abusers, no longer see themselves as deficient, their desire to act out is more and more diminished. This is where the work of the inquiries lies.

Zan: I remember that when I was twenty years old, I had a crush on a ten-year-old girl. Lots of sexual fantasies about that. But I put it out of my mind. At the age of thirty-five, fantasies about young girls came back. And now they're very powerful. I'm actually afraid that I'm going to act on them. When my young niece is around, I can't stop the thoughts about wanting to be intimate with her.

Scott: I want you to imagine yourself sitting in a circle, with young girls all around you. How do you feel as you think about acting out?

Zan: Excited. Powerful. Alive. And also scared that I'm going to act out.

Scott: Now imagine being unable to act out with any of these girls. There you are, sitting in the middle of the circle by yourself, unable to do anything. How do you feel about yourself? What deficiency story is operating?

Zan: Powerless. I feel really alone—depressed, actually. I can see that I'm trying to feel better or more powerful through these fantasies.

Scott: Trying to cover up the pain?

Zan: Yes.

Scott: Let's not cover it up with the fantasies. Instead, I want you to try to find this powerless self.

	Stop focusing on the girls as a way to medicate your pain. Where is that powerless self?
Zan:	Right here—it's me. I've felt that way ever since I was sexually abused as a child.
Scott:	Are the words "right here—it's me" you, the powerless self?
Zan:	Yes.
Scott:	This means that there's some emotion or sensation arising. That's the pain you're trying to medicate. Would you agree?
Zan:	Yes. Feels like a black hole in my stomach.
Scott:	Are the words "feels like a black hole in my stomach" you, the powerless self?
Zan:	No.
Scott:	I want you to observe that black hole without describing it in words.
Zan:	OK.
Scott:	Do you see it?
Zan:	Yes.
Scott:	Is that picture of the black hole the powerless you?
Zan:	When I'm not describing it that way? No, it's a picture.
Scott:	When you look right at the surface of that picture, does it have the words "I'm powerless" written on it?

Zan:	No.
Scott:	Stop and listen to that picture, as odd as that sounds. Is that picture talking? Is it saying, "I'm powerless"?
Zan:	No.
Scott:	Observe that picture directly, without words, and watch it begin to change on its own. Tell me what happens.
Zan:	It's starting to fade. But a picture of me as a little boy is showing up now.
Scott:	Are the words "a picture of me as a little boy is showing up now" you, the powerless self?
Zan:	No. The words aren't, but the picture itself is me.
Scott:	Are the words "the picture itself is me" you, the powerless self? I want you to look just at the words themselves, as if there's a typewriter in your mind spelling out the words.
Zan:	Those are just words.
Scott:	Stare at the picture of that boy, without words. What happens?
Zan:	It fades. Now I feel a deep sadness.
Scott:	Are the words "I feel a deep sadness" the powerless you?
Zan:	No. But now I want to focus back on those girls. I can see that I use those fantasies to medicate the sadness.

Scott:	Don't medicate the sadness. Feel it, without words and pictures.
Zan:	[*long pause*] OK…this hurts.
Scott:	Are the words "this hurts" the powerless self?
Zan:	No. The energy is moving through now. It feels quite peaceful as I just let it be there.
Scott:	Then just sit with that energy for a while, without going back to words and pictures.
Zan:	Feels good to just let it be there.
Scott:	Is that energy the powerless you?
Zan:	No.
Scott:	How about the words "I'm powerless"? Are those words you?
Zan:	Yes.
Scott:	Look back at the young girls. Is there a drive to imagine acting out again?
Zan:	Yes, to cover this pain.
Scott:	The pain is arising because of identification with certain words you carry about yourself. Don't cover the pain. Go deeply into it, without words and pictures.
Zan:	I see that as the pain dissolves through observing it, the drive to act out releases, too. I'm a predator.

Scott:	Are the words "I'm a predator" the powerless self?
Zan:	Society makes me feel that way, as if there's something inherently wrong with me for feeling the way I do and wanting to act out.
Scott:	Are the words "society makes me feel that way, as if there's something inherently wrong with me" you—the powerless man?
Zan:	No.
Scott:	How about the words "I'm a predator"?
Zan:	There's a lot of pain with those words.
Scott:	So you think those words are you?
Zan:	Yes.
Scott:	Sit with the energy of that pain, without labels. Let it arise and fall, without trying to medicate it, understand it, or go back to labels about yourself. Is that energy the powerless you?
Zan:	No, it's not me. Just energy. And it's relaxing.
Scott:	Scan the circle of girls again. Does that powerless self appear again?
Zan:	Yes—when I see my niece.
Scott:	Is the picture of your niece the powerless self?
Zan:	No. But I see myself acting out with her.
Scott:	Is that picture of you acting out with her the powerless self?

Zan:	No, it's just a mental image. But it brings up excited feelings.
Scott:	Are the words "it brings up excited feelings" you?
Zan:	No.
Scott:	Let those excited feelings arise, without labeling them or doing anything with them. Let them wash through naturally.
Zan:	They're gone. And the pain isn't there, either.
Scott:	Scan the circle again. Does the powerless you seem to arise again?
Zan:	I see my uncle in the circle. He sexually abused me. And I instantly feel powerless again.
Scott:	Is that picture of your uncle the powerless you?
Zan:	No, that's a picture of him.
Scott:	Look directly at the mental picture of him abusing you, as painful as it may be. Is that picture the powerless you?
Zan:	Yes, definitely!
Scott:	Again, that means emotion or sensation is arising with the words. And the emotion or sensation feels welded together with that picture. Stare at that picture directly, without interpreting it, until it falls away. Then sit with that energy in the body, letting it be exactly as it is. No words or pictures added to it.

Zan:	Intense sadness.
Scott:	Are the words "intense sadness" you, the powerless person?
Zan:	No.
Scott:	Feel the energy without those words added to it.
Zan:	This is such a release. I've been avoiding this pain. It's moving through now. It's OK to be with this pain. I didn't know that it was OK until now.
Scott:	The nameless, pictureless energy that's moving through—is that the powerless self?
Zan:	No, it's not. And I can't find that self.
Scott:	Scan the circle of girls and your uncle. Does that powerless self arise again?
Zan:	No. It's not here.
Scott:	Is your desire to act out with those girls still here?
Zan:	No, it's gone. I can see that when I'm allowing the pain, being with it, I don't need to medicate it with the fantasies.
Scott:	Right. As you said, the desire to act out arises out of a need to medicate the pain. But when you sit with the pain, it washes through.
Zan:	This is powerful. Very powerful. I've tried so many techniques, but none of them go this deep.
Scott:	Your work is to do the Panorama Inquiry each time you feel a desire to act out. Immediately stop

focusing on the object of your desire, and try instead to find the powerless you.

Zan: Wow! Yes, what a tool. I will do that. This is about me, not them.

Scott: It's about a *you* that's an illusion. You've believed a lie about yourself for years—that you're powerless. Can you find that person now?

Zan: No...no...I can't find him. I feel completely at ease, as if there's nothing outside myself that can truly medicate this pain.

Scott: Right. The belief in yourself as deficient is what drives the acting out and the fantasizing. Even if you act out, it's only a temporary fix for the pain. With any temporary fix, the deficiency story will pop up again after the fix is over, making you want to act out again and again. This is why your work is to see through that story and be with the pain.

Zan: Makes logical sense.

Scott: It does make logical sense. But you want to go deeper than logic. Actually try to find that powerless self whenever you see yourself fantasizing and trying to medicate the pain.

Zan: I see what you're saying. The mind can only take me so far. This isn't about logic, really. It's about seeing through this lie I carry about myself.

Scott: Exactly. See through it each time it arises. That's where the healing is.

More About Being an Abuser

As with other dialogues presented in this book, the above compresses a longer, less smooth series of dialogues into its most relevant points. It was a difficult one for him, and for me, full of silences and false starts. We sat with these, and persevered, very much to Zan's credit. I did not ascertain during this process whether Zan had acted out on his impulses, and I do not wish to frame him as a stand-in for all individuals struggling with such impulses. But it seemed to me Zan felt the danger he posed to his niece, and he was desperate for some way to reduce it. Zan emerged from this dialogue having made contact with his own deficiency story, and having twice perceived the connection between his powerless and deficient feelings and his fantasies about sexual contact with children. He was not instantly relieved of his impulses or his sense of self deficiency or his pain. But he had a crucial insight into the roots of his urges, and it was a tool he could work with both to keep himself from abusing a child as he had been abused, and to heal himself.

Our work as human beings is to see through and heal this deep sense of deficiency, however or wherever it shows up. Many people who abuse others do not, cannot, or will not see that their actions come from a sense of deficiency and separation. Not seeing this, they may not be open to the inquiries in this book. If they are, though, there is a potential for prevention that goes beyond what internal shame, social stigmatization, and incarceration can yield. In all cases, victims have to be protected and abusers punished for their crimes. In some cases, deep inquiry may halt an abusive cycle and offer healing to victims and abusers alike.

If You Heal Yourself, You Heal All Relationships

When you heal yourself, you heal all relationships. You heal the world because the world you see is a product of your own words, pictures, and energies. The more we create an atmosphere in which everyone—the one who abuses and the one who is abused—feels free and safe looking inward at these deficiency stories, the more we create an overall atmosphere of compassionate healing. We're all in this together. These inquiries can be done in conjunction with therapy, programs in prison or rehabilitation programs, victim advocacy or assistance programs, and other healing measures. When our focus is on healing this sense of deficiency in all of us, we'll use whatever works. The well-being of all humans, and of all life, is that important. This becomes even more apparent when we see through deficiency and separation as it arises in each of us.

CHAPTER 11

Overcompensation

Sometimes the core deficiency story is so painful that we conceal it from others and ourselves. We act as if the opposite of the deficiency story were true. The mind overcompensates in an effort for us not to feel the painful emotions that lie at the core of the deficiency story.

When we overcompensate, what's actually going on is self-deception. We convince ourselves that we're more worthy, special, important, knowledgeable, or spiritual than others, and we hide behind this façade. Others then appear in the mirror of relationship as less worthy, less special, less important, less knowledgeable, or less spiritual.

When we're truly free of the core belief *I'm deficient*, we find no reason to overcompensate. We feel little need to identify with the stories *I'm good* or *I'm worthy*, or to define others as bad or unworthy. When we're free of the belief in separation and deficiency, we naturally radiate that freedom, which may make us seem confident but not arrogant. There's nothing to brag about, because we're no longer trying to convince anyone of anything.

When overcompensation is present, there are two ways for you to uncover it and see through it while doing the inquiries:

1. Overcompensating means keeping painful emotions buried by telling yourself that you're better than others in

some way. But those emotions usually arise along with painful memories. So if you want to uncover and see through overcompensation, remember a time when you felt deficient. Sit with that memory until painful emotions arise. Then ask yourself, "What are these painful emotions saying about me?"

2. When you're doing the Panorama Inquiry, imagine others in your life in a circle around you, and notice how you define them as somehow less important than you. Then imagine that there's no one and nothing in the circle around you. In that moment, you won't be using the mirror of relationship to define yourself in relation to other people, and this shift will tend to reveal that you—by yourself, in the absence of others who are supposedly less important—do not exist as someone who is more important. That's because everything is in relationship—depending on its context for meaning—and so identities like *I'm more important* begin to fall apart when you have no one with whom to compare yourself.

Using the Panorama Inquiry for Overcompensation

Ray: This may sound arrogant, but I don't feel I'm deficient at all. I think I'm really special, frankly.

Scott: Are the words "I'm really special" you, the special person?

Ray: No, they're just words. But they're words about me, and I feel that they're true.

Scott:	Pull up a memory of a time when you didn't feel special.
Ray:	Got it…when I got fired from my job.
Scott:	Does that bring up any painful emotions?
Ray:	Yes—something feels off in my stomach.
Scott:	When you sit here, playing that memory over and over, and staying with that feeling, do you feel special?
Ray:	No, I feel awful. I felt like a loser back then. I want to put that out of my mind.
Scott:	And go back to thinking you're special?
Ray:	I see your point.
Scott:	That's overcompensation. It's great to feel good about yourself and even love yourself. But when you tell a story that's merely hiding pain, you bring disharmony to your relationships. Think about all the people in your life you've treated as being less than you.
Ray:	Yes. I have treated people that way. Ask my ex-wife. She would love this if she were here.
Scott:	Imagine a circle in which you're surrounded by all the people you've defined as less than you. What do those people mirror back to you about yourself?
Ray:	That I'm special. I can see that I'm defining all of them as if there's something wrong with them.

Scott:	Now eliminate the circle. Imagine there are no people around you at all. Can you feel special without those others to define yourself against?
Ray:	Yes, I feel special.
Scott:	Compared to whom?
Ray:	Well, for example, compared to a friend of mine who hasn't accomplished much at all in his life.
Scott:	See how you had to bring someone back into the circle so you could feel special?
Ray:	Yes.
Scott:	This time, I would like you to imagine there's really no one else around you. Just let your mind be quiet with regard to all the others in your life.
Ray:	This is really hard. I want to go back to comparing myself. This is actually really scary.
Scott:	What does that feeling seem to indicate about you?
Ray:	That I'm insignificant.
Scott:	Maybe that's the core story. You named it.
Ray:	It is. I know it is.
Scott:	Add someone into the circle who doesn't believe you're special.
Ray:	My ex-wife. My father.
Scott:	What do they mirror back to you about yourself? Who are you in relation to them?

Ray:	Insignificant, especially with my father. I could never gain his approval.
Scott:	Can you find that insignificant self?
Ray:	Yes. I'm feeling that right now.
Scott:	Where is it?
Ray:	I remember sitting on the couch when I was a kid and hearing my father yell, "You're not worth a damn thing!"
Scott:	Is that mental picture you, the insignificant self? Take your time.
Ray:	[crying] Yes. That's me.
Scott:	I want you to look directly at that picture, without adding any words to it. Just watch it fade away on its own. Then bring attention into your body, without thoughts. Feel the energy that's there.
Ray:	I feel it. I'm angry.
Scott:	Are the words "I'm angry" the insignificant self?
Ray:	No.
Scott:	Feel the energy without words and pictures. Is that energy you?
Ray:	No, it's just energy. Feels good to finally experience it. I know it's been there awhile... now I'm thinking about my divorce from my ex-wife.
Scott:	Is that picture you, the insignificant person?

Ray:	No.
Scott:	Can you find the insignificant self?
Ray:	No.
Scott:	Can you find the really special self?
Ray:	No, I just feel love.
Scott:	Notice that when you're gut-level honest like this, willing to look at whatever deficiency is causing you to overcompensate, a greater freedom shows up.
Ray:	Absolutely. I'm feeling no need to tell myself I'm special.
Scott:	Or to judge others in the opposite way.

More About Overcompensation

Overcompensation can be tricky to spot. Authentic confidence expresses itself naturally. It never has to announce itself by saying, "Look how great I am!" To spot overcompensation, we need to look for ways in which our beliefs about ourselves, such as *I'm more important*, carry with them a sense of doubt or fear under the surface. If we were truly confident and feeling good about ourselves, we wouldn't need to be defensive at all, but doubt or fear appears when someone challenges that belief in our importance.

When we defend an inflated or falsely positive self-image, we use the mind to protect a false identity. We try to convince ourselves and others that we're better, more worthy, or more important than they are, and we're probably not conscious of the doubt, fear, and insecurity underlying that self-image. But in the moment of being attacked, we become sensitive, and that tells us everything we need to know: We're overcompensating; there's a sense of core deficiency underneath all the posturing.

What should you do when you see yourself defending an inflated or falsely positive self-image? Don't judge yourself for it. That just feeds the underlying story *There's something wrong with me*. Instead, when your self-image is attacked, make the underlying doubt, fear, or insecurity conscious as a bodily sensation. Really feel it. Let it flow through, without adding words or pictures to it. When your self-image begins to crumble, what you experience can feel like the fear of death, and almost everything in your system may want to avoid facing such a strong feeling. This is why so much energy goes into keeping the false self-image alive. Keeping it going feels like a matter of survival.

Vulnerability is often thought of as weakness, especially in men. But when you're vulnerable, you're open to being triggered in relationship, and you're open to facing the doubt, fear, or insecurity that keeps a false self-image in place. Vulnerability allows you to transform and move out of a limiting self-identity. When you face your painful feelings directly, you no longer have to maintain a false self-image as a way to overcompensate for them. The self-image is then seen as illusory—as just a passing set of words. Your true power lies in openhearted vulnerability.

Authentic confidence doesn't have its basis in any self-image. When you come to know this for yourself, you will probably experience a natural, unmanufactured confidence. But when you rely on an inflated or falsely positive self-image like *I'm more important*, that self-image can exist only for as long as you continue to define yourself against others whom you see as less important than you are. A manufactured story must be defended at all costs precisely because it is a lie. The lie protects you from feeling your underlying doubt, fear, or insecurity. Authentic, unmanufactured confidence never has to defend itself.

CHAPTER 12

Helping

Helping others might be considered one of the most virtuous human actions, especially when it's performed selflessly, with no expectation of anything in return. Yet helping so often has some personal agenda behind it. We may not even realize we're expecting something in return, such as praise, acknowledgment, personal validation, or love. When we operate with expectations like these, we invite suffering into our relationships. The core deficiency story that's operating in this situation is *I'm not lovable* or *I'm not valid*. And so, by helping others, we seek love and validation from them. We may even try to control them or manipulate them into acknowledging our helpfulness: *How can you treat me like this after all I've done for you?*

Using the Boomerang Inquiry for Helping

Sandra: I've been helping my mother clean her house and take care of her personal matters since her divorce from my father. I know I'm doing it out of love. How can helping my mother be coming from a sense of deficiency?

Scott:	It may not be coming from deficiency at all. You may just love helping your mother. Let's try the Boomerang Inquiry. Use the mirror. When you look at your mother, does that bring up any trigger, like emotional pain?
Sandra:	Not really, until I imagine her not saying, "Thank you." She doesn't say it much at all. It's very selfish of her.
Scott:	Remember a time when she didn't thank you after you helped her. What does that bring up in you?
Sandra:	I'm hurt. It feels like she doesn't love me, even though I know she does.
Scott:	Good—you've named it. Can you find the one who is unlovable? Are the words "she doesn't thank me" it?
Sandra:	No.
Scott:	But did your body react in some way when you heard yourself say those words?
Sandra:	Yes—sadness.
Scott:	Is the word "sadness" the one who is unlovable? Look right at the word itself.
Sandra:	No—not me.
Scott:	Bring your attention into your body, and feel the sadness without calling it anything. Is that energy the one who is unlovable?

Sandra:	Yes, that's me.
Scott:	What words or pictures are coming up with that energy?
Sandra:	I see a memory of my father ignoring me when I was little.
Scott:	Is that picture, by itself, the one who is unlovable?
Sandra:	Yes.
Scott:	Put it into a picture frame in your mind.
Sandra:	I can see now it's just a memory. It's not me. I feel like the unlovable me is right here.
Scott:	Where is it? Look for it.
Sandra:	It's this energy. It's in my chest.
Scott:	Can you see any shape or form around that energy, like a picture of your chest or anything else?
Sandra:	I don't see a picture of my chest. I see a heart, and it looks like it's locked up, like it can't open.
Scott:	Is that mental picture you, the one who is unlovable?
Sandra:	No, but it seems to belong to me, the one who is unlovable.
Scott:	We aren't looking for things that belong to her. We're looking for *her*. Is that picture her?
Sandra:	It's fading now. No, it's not her.
Scott:	Where are you, the one who is unlovable?

Sandra: I see the thought *Mom is selfish.* But that's not me. I can't find it.

Scott: Just rest, soaking in the experience of not being able to find the one who is unlovable.

Sandra: I feel warmth in my heart. But I can see that's not me, either. It's just a really open, warm space, almost impersonal. Very loving. I've been trying to get love from my mother, even though I already know she loves me. Somehow it wasn't enough just to know that in my mind. I didn't feel it.

Scott: Look back at your mother. Is that picture the one who is unlovable?

Sandra: No, I can see her not thanking me. And there's nothing wrong with her, or me. It's all so silly now. I can see that.

Scott: Anytime you feel triggered when you're helping others and they don't appreciate it, you can look and see that you're buying into that core story again. And then look for it, just like we did today.

Sandra It no longer makes any sense to expect my mother to give me what she can't give me. She can only be herself. It's me. This is all about me.

Scott: Can you find that *me?*

Sandra: Ha-ha! No. What a relief! I feel such a deep love right now.

Scott: It's painful to think that we lack love, and that only someone else can give it to us.

More About Helping

There are often mixed motives operating in us when we're helping. For example, there may be a part of us that just selflessly loves helping others. Along with that, we may also be seeking validation or love through our helpful actions. We may not even be able to detect that we're seeking these things until we don't get what we want. Subtle resentments may start to develop. We may find ourselves weaving stories about someone we're helping: *He doesn't appreciate all that I do!* These resentments and stories are indicators that part of our motive for helping is to seek validation or love. *He doesn't appreciate me* really means *I'm not loved* or *I'm not valid.*

It can be difficult to see that the issue doesn't lie with the people we're helping. They're only mirrors for the belief in deficiency in ourselves. When other people don't appreciate our efforts or help us in return, that core wound of deficiency comes up. It's the fuel for our resentment. And the more invalid or unlovable we feel, the more we seek validity and love from others. Helping then becomes a seeking game—a continuous pattern of looking outside ourselves for what we believe we lack within.

How can you come to see whether, at least in part, you're helping others from a sense of deficiency in yourself? Easy—do the inquiries! They're designed to reveal how deficiency shows up in relationship, and to bring up the emotional pain of what it's like not to get what you're seeking—love or validation. They're designed to penetrate that story and the pain. And as the story is seen through, selfless service begins to appear more automatically. You find yourself wanting to help, regardless of whether others appreciate your actions or help you in return.

A few years ago, I was working with a man named Eric on his constant need to help others. Eric became pretty angry and defensive with me as I brought up the possibility that his constant desire to help might be coming from a belief in self-deficiency. He said things like "But helping is always good, so it doesn't matter why I do it" and "The world needs more people like me who are just trying to love and take care of others."

Those sound like reasonable statements. But Eric was suffering on some level. That's why he'd contacted me in the first place. He couldn't connect the dots. He'd been working as a caretaker for years, but despite all those years of what he considered selfless service, he was deeply unsatisfied with life.

Eric became so reluctant to engage with me during his session that he refused at first to do the inquiries. He didn't want to look directly at the core story and the pain that were driving him as a caretaker. A willingness to look finally opened up in Eric once I explained to him that I help people on a daily basis and have had to look into whether there are selfish motives operating in me. Because I was transparent with him about my own life and work, he felt safe enough to do the Panorama Inquiry. He was amazed to see that he had been feeling invalid and unlovable from an early age. It had started with his parents. As we did the inquiry, he noticed that, to one degree or another, he was holding on to resentment toward many of the people he had helped over the years. When he became able to point back toward himself, instead of outward toward others, and when it became possible for him to name the deficiency story—*I'm invalid and unlovable*—the inquiry began to open him up to new insights.

The more he sat with the pain of resentment, without labeling it, the more the pain started to feel like a warm bath of love. The love was almost too much for him at first, and he would scurry back into the story of how others did not appreciate him. Finally, though, he saw that the whole story of being invalid and unlovable was an empty lie.

After working with me, Eric reported that he was continuing to do the inquiry for all his relationships. He noticed that some of his helpful actions had been quite aggressive before he learned to do the inquiry. In the past, he would literally force his help on others, even when they hadn't asked for it. But now he can allow pain to be as it is, without adding stories and labels to it, and he is experiencing love as the natural state of presence itself, as the alive spaciousness within the body. Now he can be much more relaxed and has no need to force his help on others. He sees now that the act of helping is most rewarding and natural when it's truly selfless, and when it's performed without any expectation of return.

True selflessness does not come from our efforts to fit the image of a helpful person, nor does it come from trying to get others to love and validate us. It arises automatically once we see through the story of deficiency. When that story is seen through, love arises not from our personal stories (which are mostly self-centered) but rather as presence itself. This is the most satisfying and validating recognition we can have. Love is revealed to be everywhere, in everything we see and in everyone we meet. We cannot "get" it. We *are* it. Love is life. It's the very nature of our experience, once we stop believing the lie *I lack love and need to get it from others.*

CHAPTER 13

Peacemaking

Many of us want harmony in our relationships as well as in the world, and both would probably be better off if more people concerned themselves with making peace instead of fomenting conflict and waging war. On the surface, peacemaking can seem virtuous, even highly spiritual or selfless. And sometimes it really is what it seems to be.

But peacemaking sometimes carries with it a personal deficiency story that drives the peacemaker to seek harmony in order to avoid anger and conflict. The story is usually some version of *I'm not loved* or *I'm unlovable*. Peacemakers frequently can't see why they have a tendency toward peacemaking—the core deficiency story is usually unconscious.

Peacemakers are often uncomfortable expressing their own viewpoints and opinions, for fear that others will react with anger or disapproval and that conflict will result. Because anger and conflict pose a particular danger to those who carry this core story, peacemakers may find themselves habitually engaging in "people pleasing" and compulsively agreeing with everyone else's viewpoint in order to avoid rocking the boat. For the peacemaker, love is equated exclusively with agreement and kindness, and so anger and fear are not loved and welcomed when they arise. Ironically, however, the peacemaker is actually at war—with conflict, anger, fear, and discomfort. And when the boat is rocked, as it inevitably is, and when conflict arises, the story *I'm unlovable* comes to the surface. But this is a deeply threatening story, and making peace becomes a way of bringing harmony to relationships in an attempt to quiet this inner self that feels unlovable, or to avoid facing it.

Using the Panorama Inquiry for Peacemaking

Geoff: I'm not exactly sure why I'm here. I just know that these inquiries can bring a lot of peace to the world, and I'm all for that.

Scott: Me, too. I value peace.

Geoff: Of course—me, too. When I look at other people arguing and fighting over who's right and who's wrong, it makes me sick to my stomach.

Scott: That's not very peaceful. Create a circle in which you are sitting in the middle. Around this circle, place all the people in your life who have been arguing and fighting. Do you see them?

Geoff: Yes. I see my mom and dad arguing. I see my brother, who's always challenging me on what I say. He seems to just want to be right all the time. I see Seth, an old friend I no longer speak to. Seth and I got into an argument one evening, and it ended badly.

Scott: Use the mirror. What do these people mirror back to you about yourself?

Geoff: That I desire peace above all else.

Scott:	But all these people in the circle are arguing and in conflict. Do you find yourself in conflict with how they're acting?
Geoff:	Yes. That's good to see.
Scott:	Sit for a moment, and just be gut-level honest. When you see conflict around you or directed toward you, does this bring up a sense that there's something wrong?
Geoff:	Yes. It feels unloving.
Scott:	Does it feel personal?
Geoff:	Yes. It brings up fear. I don't want to be around them. So, yes—when they're in conflict, especially with me, I feel, frankly, as if they don't like me. I don't feel loved.
Scott:	Let's try to find that unlovable self. Look at the memory of your mom and dad arguing. Is that mental picture you, the unlovable self?
Geoff:	Yes. I'm not even in the picture, but somehow that's me. Weird—I have that sick feeling in my stomach now.
Scott:	Are the words "I have that sick feeling in my stomach now" you?
Geoff:	No, they're just words describing the unlovable self.
Scott:	In this inquiry, we want to stick to finding this unlovable self, not just words that describe it. Let that memory of your mom and dad relax and fade

away, as well as those words. Is that energy in your body you, the unlovable self? Just observe the energy. Don't think about it.

Geoff: No. It's dissipating now.

Scott: Look back at that mental picture of your mom and dad. Is that you?

Geoff: No.

Scott: Scan the circle, and let me know when you feel triggered, when that sense of being unlovable pops up again.

Geoff: As much as I don't want to revisit that argument with Seth, it's coming up.

Scott: In words or pictures?

Geoff: Both. I see myself trying to avoid him. And I'm thinking *He needs to work on his anger.* I'm definitely not at peace with him.

Scott: Are the words "He needs to work on his anger" you, the unlovable self?

Geoff: No. Frankly, I don't even know if I feel unlovable at the core. I just sometimes feel rejected or excluded when others are mean.

Scott: That's OK. If that core story is not operating, this inquiry won't harm anything. You'll just find that it wasn't useful. Look at the memory of you trying to avoid Seth. Is that picture you, the unlovable self?

Geoff: I know it's just a memory. But I'm feeling fear. So I'll say yes.

Scott: It's always good to say yes when your body is reacting to a thought. Is the word "fear" you?

Geoff: No. I can feel that fear now, without many words attached to it. That energy is not me. It just came and went.

Scott: Scan the circle again.

Geoff: I can see something else in the circle now—my colleagues at work, in a heated discussion. I'm there being quiet and feeling uncomfortable.

Scott: "I'm there being quiet and feeling uncomfortable." Are those words you, the unlovable self?

Geoff: Yes—the whole scene looks pretty crazy. Lots of conflict.

Scott: Let all those words relax, even the word "uncomfortable." Can you just sit and feel that discomfort without trying to change it or label it?

Geoff: Yes. But that feels like me.

Scott: That just means some words or pictures are arising.

Geoff: The words "I don't want to do this." Those words keep repeating themselves in my mind, over and over, as I try to just observe the energy in my body, without thoughts. They seem to keep getting louder and louder.

Scott:	Put those words in a picture frame in your mind. Look right at the picture. Are those words you?
Geoff:	No. OK…now the words fell away. Let me sit with this pain. The discomfort is just there, not doing anything. Just energy. And now it's expanding into space, diminishing. It's not me, the unlovable self. It has no story attached to it at all right now.
Scott:	Can you find that unlovable person right here, right now?
Geoff:	No, and as I scan the circle again and see people arguing, it just seems OK as it is. There's nothing to get worked up about. I can see that I've been at war with war, in conflict with conflict. I want people to like me. And when they're upset or angry, I feel rejected.
Scott:	Yes—unlovable.
Geoff:	I can also see that I've been misunderstanding what love really is, as if it's only there when everyone is agreeing with everyone else, and when no one is challenging me.
Scott:	Right.
Geoff:	Love is just here. It's not just a loving feeling. I'm seeing that even conflict and discomfort are OK. It's all love, somehow.
Scott:	Sometimes conflict can be the very thing that wakes us up from certain stories we're holding on to about ourselves.

Geoff:	Yeah—the story *They don't love me*. I can't find that person. I didn't even know that story was operating. What a blind spot!
Scott:	Just remember that if you find yourself making peace again and avoiding conflict, that old script may be running. When the core story is *I'm unlovable*, people seek agreement, surface-level kindness, and peace as a way to feel loved. But it doesn't really work, because in reality, conflict happens.
Geoff:	Yes. I've been at war with conflict, especially when it involves me directly.
Scott:	Many peacemakers wage a kind of war against conflict. Notice that when peacemaking comes from the core belief *I'm unlovable*, it's also often centered on a war with basic emotions inside you, like fear and anger. Conflict brings up those emotions. And when those emotions arise, they're considered non-peaceful emotions.
Geoff:	How can it be true peace if there's a war inside me against these emotions? This inquiry shows me that these emotions can be totally welcomed. I just didn't see that I was trying to make peace in order to feel love. That's just a surface-level peace, a way to try to protect myself from feeling.
Scott:	Yes, and when you aren't at war with these emotions, and when they're allowed to arise freely, the emotions themselves are seen to be loved.
Geoff:	[*long pause*] I'm speechless…I just don't have any words for how open and loving I feel right now.

Facing the Core Emotional Wound

Notice that when Geoff began to feel, without words, the discomfort in his body, his mind kept shouting *I don't want to do this*, over and over. This is very common in these inquiries. The core deficiency story strikes at the very heart of who we think we are. In many of our relationships, it often operates under the radar. We can't see it directly, because we're too busy pointing outward toward others. We're constantly deflecting attention from the core pain that holds the story together. Here, Geoff had been busy pointing toward all the others who were in conflict. He'd been affected by a blind spot, unable to see the story *I'm unlovable* directly. But as we began to inquire into that core deficiency story, thoughts came screaming to the surface, as if to say *No, no! You can't take this central story from me. This is who I really am.*

This is the mind's way of overcompensating for emotions. Frankly, it can feel safer to point outward and stay locked in mental viewpoints than to actually sit with the emotional pain that lies at the center of the deficiency story. But these inquiries are designed to make that emotional pain conscious. The more conscious the pain becomes, and the more freely it's allowed to flow—without the mind's effort to overcompensate—the less power the story retains.

In my work with people from all over the world, people from many different cultural and personal backgrounds, I've noticed that one thing humans have in common is difficulty in just sitting and feeling painful emotions without labeling them. So many of us learn in childhood that painful emotions are bad. We're told to think positively, go out and play, or otherwise distract ourselves from emotional pain. Young boys are often told that boys don't cry, as if sadness, rather than being a natural human emotion, were a weakness having to do with gender.

Parents often react with discipline, scorn, or judgment when their children have tantrums, and in this way they signal that the feelings arising in their children are bad and should be suppressed. Parents rarely deal directly with their children's fear of death when it arises, or even with anxiety around things like illness, bullying at school, and athletic or educational performance. Instead of teaching their children to let fear arise freely, without overcompensation from the mind, parents are often quick to soothe the fear. All of this creates an atmosphere in which painful emotions are repressed or suppressed in childhood. As we grow into adults, we rely mostly on thinking. We intellectualize and think our way through life, avoiding the more primal emotional energies that lie at the core of our personal stories, and that arise when we're triggered in relationship. Many people then turn to addictive substances and activities as a way to cope with basic human emotions that they haven't learned how to feel directly.

It's no wonder so many people eventually seek self-improvement, recovery, religion, or what some call *enlightenment*. In this atmosphere, where so often the direct experience of emotions is avoided, it's only natural for humans to seek such ways to cope. For example, in my work with seekers, I've noticed that many treat enlightenment as a way not to have to feel emotions. They dream of a perfect state of peace or bliss in which they will no longer be triggered emotionally or feel sad, angry, or fearful. But what, really, is enlightenment? It's the seeing through of ego— that sense of a separate, deficient self. The seeing through of this separate, deficient self is a *present* seeing, a seeing based in the alive inner spaciousness that I call *presence*. That's how I define enlightenment. And that's what these inquiries are designed to reveal. When you can't find the deficient self, you experience life free from identification with the words, pictures, and energies that are now, presently, arising.

But this is where it gets tricky. Enlightenment, in this sense, is not a way to avoid present feelings. It's the complete *allowing of* those feelings to be as they are. Once we're not labeling the feelings and going back into the story, the energy of emotion is allowed to flow freely. All the mind's strategies fall away in that moment. We're finally able to be with our pain instead of avoiding it by relying on the intellect or pointing outward toward others, as if they were the source of the pain. We are responsible for our own well-being. When we're clear, our relationships clear up.

People often start doing the inquiries with the assumption that I am going to help them find a way to avoid having to feel the darkest emotional energies within them. They are surprised to find instead that the inquiries direct them to fully face those energies. Notice that Geoff, for instance, was avoiding certain emotions. His mind tried to put up a block. Once he saw that the words were not himself, he was able to sit and allow the emotions to be as they were, without labels. This is how the healing happens. The freedom Geoff experienced near the end of the inquiry was due to recognition of a fundamental rest in which all words, pictures, and energies arise and fall freely, without identification. In allowing the emotions to be as they were, he was no longer overcompensating with the mind. He was finally able to face the emotional pain that lay at the core of the story *I'm unlovable*. He saw through his peacemaking efforts, which were largely an attempt to avoid inner pain and to make "peace" as a way to feel loved. Geoff was excited after this inquiry. He e-mailed me over and over to let me know that he was experiencing a deeper, selfless peace that was not at war with emotional pain or conflict. For a while, he said, he had continued to see his mind wanting to make peace as a way to overcompensate for the uncomfortable feelings that arose in the face of conflict, but at some point he no longer needed to do the inquiry. He began to feel emotions directly, as soon as they arose. Once emotions are allowed to come and go freely in awareness, the mind naturally begins to quiet around the core deficiency story. The need to overcompensate diminishes. As a result, the inquiry is no longer needed.

CHAPTER 14

Abandonment

Fear of abandonment is a common issue. It usually stems from childhood experiences of having parents or other significant figures be absent physically, psychologically, or emotionally. The core deficiency story is *I'm abandoned* or *I'm not supported*. Like all deficiency scripts, the story of being abandoned is an interpretation of a self that feels deficient. The deficient self sees most situations and the actions of others through a lens of deficiency so that the truth of that story seems to be confirmed.

When this core idea is operating, relationships can be a source of real suffering, as if no one were really there for you. And when someone appears to leave your life—through a breakup, divorce, conflict, or death—the core story can come screaming to the surface. This apparent abandonment may prompt you to look for someone else who can cover up the pain. But the pattern often repeats, and when the new person leaves or is emotionally unavailable or unsupportive, the wound reappears.

Using the Boomerang Inquiry for Abandonment

No one can abandon you unless you buy into the fiction *I'm an abandoned person*. In this example, Sarah worked through the inquiry by herself. She had noticed her core abandonment story and decided to use the Boomerang Inquiry. This is what she wrote:

> I can't believe he left me. A ten-year relationship, and he just leaves, without even saying why. I feel so alone. I'm never going to be in a relationship with a man again.
>
> *Use the mirror:* He is mirroring back to me that I'm alone. This is what I really believe I am.
>
> *Name it:* Abandoned self.
>
> Are the words "I can't believe he left me" it?
>
> No.
>
> Are the words "he just leaves, without even saying why" me, the abandoned self?
>
> Yes, that's me. I'm sad.
>
> Are the words "I'm sad" me?
>
> No. [*Here, Sarah rested, feeling the emotion directly, without words or pictures.*]
>
> This energy is not the abandoned self.
>
> Where is it?
>
> "I'm alone." Yes, that's it. [*Here, she rested again, without words or pictures, feeling the emotion.*]
>
> No, that feeling is not it. [*She rested yet again, looking for that self.*]
>
> I can't find it.

Doing the Inquiries by Yourself

Sarah's inquiry was fairly short. It didn't take her long to see through the core deficiency story. That story may arise for her again, but she can use one of the inquiries to look into the unfindability of the abandoned self.

Sometimes the looking has to go deeper and take longer. When you're doing the inquiries on your own, you'll know which words, pictures, and energies to observe. It's all in your own direct experience. And you'll know when you've seen the emptiness of the self that you're looking for. If you have difficulty doing the inquiries on your own, try writing them down or finding a partner to ask the questions.

CHAPTER 15

Control

The desire to control others doesn't just arise out of the blue. It has its roots in a particular core story about a deficient self. This story is usually some variant of *I'm afraid*, *I'm powerless*, or *I'm weak*. As in most other core deficiency stories, the focus is often turned outward in an attempt to monitor, meddle, and fix other people and life situations as a way of protecting the core story about being afraid, powerless, or weak.

We don't necessarily intend to be controlling. It just happens automatically and unconsciously as a way for us to cope with the sense of core deficiency. All the outward pointing keeps the core deficient self hidden from view. It's easier to be the boss of life than to be vulnerable and face the sense of powerlessness within. We believe we cannot be at peace unless we keep the underlying fear and sense of powerlessness at bay.

Our relationships tend to support our controlling behavior. We may find ourselves surrounded by people who depend on us and cannot function without our support. At the same time, we often engage with people who resent us and complain that we need to mind our own business and stop trying to fix them.

Using the Panorama Inquiry for Control

Michael noticed that he was triggered by his mother, his son, and his wife. After working in a number of sessions with me, he decided to do the Panorama Inquiry on his own.

> My mother has to change the way she's handling her finances. I've got to make my son attend the state university instead of community college. And I'm not going to let my wife interfere with any of this. That's how it's going to be. [*He put his mother, his son, and his wife in the circle and scanned around.*]
>
> What is my mother mirroring back to me?
>
> I'm a control freak. I know that.
>
> I feel a lot of fear in my body right now. To be honest, I'm afraid. And fear always makes me feel as if I'm really powerless over all this.
>
> *Name it:* I hate being powerless.
>
> *Find it:* Can I find the powerless self? [*He looked at the memory of his son telling him he wanted to attend community college.*]
>
> That's not me. [*He saw the words "My mother has to change."*]
>
> That's not the powerless me. [*He rested. A picture of his wife interfering came up.*]
>
> That's me, wanting to stop her.
>
> Are the words "I want to stop her" this powerless self?
>
> Yes. [*He felt the fear as energy, without words or pictures.*]

That energy is not me. [*He looked at the words "I'm afraid."*]

Yes, that's me. [*He felt the fear and watched it fall away, with no story attached to it.*]

That energy is not me.

Let me scan the circle. My mother is there. She's a trigger. I can see myself feeling weak around her as a child.

Is that picture me?

Yes. [*He observed the picture of himself as a child until it faded, and then he felt the energy.*]

That energy isn't me. [*He scanned the circle once more.*]

No trigger. I can't find the powerless self. Now I see no reason to control anyone or anything.

More About Control

All Michael had to do was stop all the outward focus and analysis of others for one moment, turn his attention inward to the fear, name the deficient self, and then try to find it. Notice that when he felt that certain words were the powerless self, he brought his attention into the body and relaxed into the energy, not feeding the energy with a story. This practice is what heals the core wound.

Michael can use this tool whenever he finds himself trying to control things. Now that he is aware of his history of controlling behavior, he can see that it isn't working. But knowing that his controlling behavior doesn't work is only half the battle. In order to see through the self that tries to control, he'll have to stop whenever he sees his controlling behavior occurring again, and he'll have to go inward to really look for the powerless self that seems to run the show.

When Michael does the inquiry, he won't be trying to change or stop his thoughts. He won't be trying to kill his mind. He won't be trying to will himself into freedom. Doing these things would just be forms of self-control, using the same mechanism of control but turning it inward instead of outward.

Nor will Michael be engaging in what's conventionally called *self-improvement*. Self-improvement often involves rearranging our core deficiency story, or devising methods to change our behavior. It may provide some relief from suffering. But it may also leave the core story *I'm powerless* lurking within. Even if Michael tries to convince himself mentally that he's not powerless, he may simply be overcompensating. He may disown his powerlessness only at the mental level while continuing to turning away from the bodily feeling of fear. As long as he takes himself to *be* any core deficiency story, he may find himself having to defend and protect that story in some way, even if he's successful at rearranging it. His efforts will only cause more disharmony in his relationships.

Instead of trying to improve his core deficiency story or control himself, Michael will be gently observing his thoughts and asking a simple question: *Is this me?* By asking that question, he'll penetrate the false belief about himself. If his thoughts then quiet, as they may do, it won't be because Michael has forced them to quiet. He will have seen that the powerless self is empty, and therefore unfindable. His present seeing will have instantly changed the way he perceives others. The mind will have naturally withdrawn from the story of a powerless self that needs to control others. He will then harmonize his relationships—the problem was never "out there."

CHAPTER 16

Hiding

Sometimes it's not clear what your core deficiency story is all about. It isn't always possible to reduce your overall sense of core deficiency to the point where it can be specifically named. Your story of psychological and emotional pain can't always be neatly placed in a particular package.

Some details of your core deficiency story inevitably emerge during an inquiry and help you see how your story shows up in your life. Remember, though, that an inquiry is not talk therapy, so don't get bogged down in either telling or analyzing your story. The point is to try to find the core deficient self, and you do that by resting and looking.

The passage that follows summarizes my work with Alexis on her vague sense that she was hiding herself. We began by using the Boomerang Inquiry. As Alexis went deeper, other people and situations began to surface in her memory, and I changed to the Panorama Inquiry. (It's absolutely fine to change the inquiry midway through if that seems appropriate—one inquiry doesn't fit all situations.) Notice that when Alexis started to analyze herself, I brought her back to the inquiry.

Using the Boomerang Inquiry and the Panorama Inquiry for a Sense of Wanting to Hide

Alexis: I don't know what to inquire into. I just can't pin it down. But I know that I've always had a feeling that I have to hide myself—that I can't show who I really am to people. I can see this in my current relationship with my boyfriend. I'm hiding myself from him.

Scott: Let's do the Boomerang Inquiry. Look at your boyfriend. Use the mirror. What does he reflect back to you about your own deficiency—about having to hide yourself?

Alexis: Vulnerability, shame, fear of being exposed. It's just the sense of wanting to hide. You see? I can't pin it down.

Scott: It's OK. You don't have to. This is your inquiry, your discovery. You know how you feel about yourself at the core. Let's just call that self something so we can move forward. Call it anything that seems to include vulnerability, shame, fear of being exposed, and the sense of wanting to hide.

Alexis: I'll just call it the hiding self, even though that doesn't sum it up completely.

Scott: Can you find that hiding self? Is the word "vulnerability" that self?

Alexis:	No. I feel a slight or vague pain with it, but it goes away quickly.
Scott:	How about the word "shame"?
Alexis:	Yes, that's me. I feel ashamed.
Scott:	Let those words relax. Bring attention into the body. Take your time, and rest. Let that energy just be there as it is. Is that energy you, the hiding self?
Alexis:	Feels like it, yes. And now all sorts of memories are popping up. I can see this little girl, me, being ridiculed as a child over and over. I can see my parents, and me as an adult not wanting to let them know about my life.
Scott:	Let's change to the Panorama Inquiry, since other people and situations are arising. Put your boyfriend, that little girl being ridiculed as a child, and your parents in a circle around you. Scan the circle. Which one triggers you the most with regard to wanting to hide?
Alexis:	The little girl.
Scott:	Look at the picture of that little girl being ridiculed. Put it in a frame. Is that you, the self who has to hide?
Alexis:	Yes. That's me. I've always felt that way. I remember being twenty and having a bunch of friends who were really open and could share anything about themselves. I just didn't want to open up. Do you think that means I'm in denial

about something? I've often thought I'm in denial. Yesterday I had that insight about denial. There must be something there. I should look into that. I also believe my boyfriend is in denial. We often don't talk a lot. We love each other, but there is a distance between us. Sometimes I'd like to know more about how he really feels, but I'm not sure I want to hear it. It might scare me. I don't know if I'm causing this distance between us or if we're both doing it. I'm starting to get really worried about our relationship as I sit and think about it now. Do you think he has a sense of wanting to hide himself, too?

Scott: I understand that it's important to talk about yourself so we can do this inquiry. But I feel you're getting off track with questions and analysis. Have you ever been able to figure those things out by constantly thinking about them?

Alexis: No. I've been thinking about this stuff for a long time, and nothing seems to really get at it.

Scott: So let's try to stick to the inquiry. Go back to the picture of the little girl being ridiculed. Is that you, the hiding self? Stick to yes or no.

Alexis: No. The picture is fading.

Scott: Scan the circle. Who triggers you?

Alexis: They're all triggering me. I see a wall between me and them.

Scott: Look directly at the wall. Can you see it?

Alexis:	Yes.
Scott:	Is that mental picture of a wall you, the hiding self?
Alexis:	No, it's a picture. The wall is more like a sense. I sense a wall there.
Scott:	OK, stare at the mental picture of the wall until it fades. Then bring your attention to the sensation that's left.
Alexis:	There is no sensation. The picture faded, and the sense of a wall faded.
Scott:	Scan the circle. Who or what triggers you?
Alexis:	My parents. I don't feel comfortable opening up to them.
Scott:	Are the words "I don't feel comfortable opening up to them" you, the self that has to hide?
Alexis:	Yes.
Scott:	Drop the words, and feel the feeling, without adding any words or pictures. Just rest into it. Is that energy you?
Alexis:	No.
Scott:	Scan the circle.
Alexis:	The little girl is coming up again, along with a memory of boys calling me "Patty Panda." I was heavy as a child.

Scott: Are the words "Patty Panda" you, the hiding self?

Alexis: I can feel a big rush of pain. Yes!

Scott: Look at the words "big rush of pain." Is that you?

Alexis: No. I'm feeling the energy now. It's just energy. It feels warm, almost nice, when I'm not calling it anything or putting it in my story.

Scott: Scan the circle.

Alexis: My boyfriend is triggering me. I feel paralyzed around him sometimes.

Scott: Look at his face. Is that picture you?

Alexis: No.

Scott: How about the words "I feel paralyzed around him sometimes"?

Alexis: Yes, that's me. That's definitely me!

Scott: Go into the body. Feel.

Alexis: Wow, my whole body is tingling. Something is releasing. It feels so good to just finally feel that. I just want to sit with that feeling.

Scott: Yes.

Alexis: That energy is not me, the hiding self.

Scott: Rest and look. Can you find that person who has to hide?

Alexis: No—no, I can't. I just feel totally open. And I can see that it's not just about wanting to hide.

I've had a story of not being worthy. And that story makes me want to hide.

Scott: Yes, sometimes it takes going through the whole inquiry before you can pinpoint that central belief about yourself. So can you find that person here who is not worthy?

Alexis: No, it's not here. I see thoughts coming and going, but no unworthy self anywhere. There's just awareness here, and it's really impersonal, transparent, and sweet. Everything is in full view—the whole story of being unworthy—but it doesn't feel like who I am. It's like a false movie, and I'm here, as awareness, looking at it.

More About Alexis's Story

Notice that Alexis couldn't pinpoint the core deficiency story *I'm unworthy* until near the end of the inquiry. That can happen. These inquiries are more art than science. If you have trouble naming the story at first, just go with whatever comes up, and work from there. The point of the inquiry is not to just put your story into a neat mental package. The point is to face the emotions that arise when you look directly at the words and pictures that you take to be who you are. Once those emotions are felt and faced, the core deficiency story often becomes clearer.

The core deficiency story *I'm unworthy* is quite common. I've worked with many people who felt that their creativity and natural expression had been stifled by fear. In my own life, I've experienced fear around expressing my viewpoints as well as around expressing myself as a musician and songwriter. That fear has paralyzed me at times.

Fully facing this fear is a doorway into letting ourselves shine as who we are. If all we do is turn away from the fear, we continue in the loop of feeling unworthy or wanting to hide. As fear is allowed to arise fully and freely, without being hooked into the core deficiency story, we're able to express ourselves more fearlessly. And even if fear arises, it becomes just another opportunity to see what we believe about ourselves.

CHAPTER 17

Seeking

Seeking in vain outside the self for what the self seems to lack is an impulse ingrained into the very fabric of the story of self. This impulse is based on one fundamental assumption: *I am separate and deficient.* We can spend our whole lives believing this basic assumption about ourselves. Until it is questioned, it tends to continue operating, driving much of what we do and how we act toward others.

When the basic assumption of separation and deficiency is undermined and seen through, fruitless seeking naturally relaxes, and we experience a stable sense of completeness with life as it is in the present moment. We can enjoy relationships, create things, express ourselves, follow our interests, and enjoy life in every way. We find that we can still move and fully operate in the world, but now without the belief that something is missing at a fundamental level.

Using the Panorama Inquiry for Futile Seeking

Tony: I can't stop seeking. I've done it all my life—looking for material items, love, sex, approval, happiness, drugs, self-improvement, and spiritual development. Nothing truly satisfies me. I'm basically seeking the future.

Scott: Put all those people and things in a circle around you, including the concept of the future. Scan the circle until you feel the seeking energy arise. That's the trigger.

Tony: They all trigger me.

Scott: What do all these people and things bring up in terms of your own deficiency? Name it. Reduce that deficiency to a particular kind of self you take yourself to be.

Tony: Incomplete.

Scott: Let's try to find the incomplete person. Are the words "I'm incomplete" you, the incomplete self?

Tony: Yes, that triggers it.

Scott: Bring attention into your body, without words. Is that energy you?

Tony: No.

Scott: Can you just let that nameless energy be there as it is?

Tony: Yes.

Scott: Is it you?

Tony: Me, the incomplete person? No.

Scott: Scan the circle until you find something in particular that brings up seeking.

Tony:	I see people in my life who don't like me. I want them to like me.
Scott:	Are the words "I see people in my life who don't like me" the incomplete person?
Tony:	No, they're just words. But when I see the face of a particular person, I feel that seeking energy.
Scott:	Is the picture of that face you, the incomplete self?
Tony:	No, and it just relaxed. It's crazy that I'm chasing pictures!
Scott:	Scan the circle.
Tony:	I used to use tobacco. I feel a pull toward going to the store to buy tobacco.
Scott:	Is the picture of tobacco the incomplete self?
Tony:	No.
Scott:	Imagine yourself driving to the store to buy tobacco. Is that picture you?
Tony:	No. It's not even happening. It's just imagination. It's not me.
Scott:	Scan the circle.
Tony:	I see a vision of other people who seem happier than I am. I want their happiness.
Scott:	Is the picture of those other people you, the incomplete person?
Tony:	No.

Scott:	How about the words "I want their happiness"?
Tony:	Just words. I can't find the incomplete person. I can't find anything to seek right now.
Scott:	Great. Scan the circle again.
Tony:	I see a picture of a spiritual teacher who looks enlightened. I want that.
Scott:	"I want to be enlightened." Are those words you, the incomplete self?
Tony:	Intellectually, I know they aren't. But something in my body wants to say yes. I'm not there yet.
Scott:	"I'm not there yet." Are those words you?
Tony:	Ha-ha! No—definitely not. And as I see that, it no longer feels like my body is saying, "I'm not there yet." The energy is there, but it doesn't feel like a big deal now. It feels OK.
Scott:	Right, because the body doesn't speak. It never says anything. There are only emotions and sensations there. It's only words and pictures that give meaning to emotions and sensations. Look at the picture of the spiritual teacher, but add no words to it. Is that picture you?
Tony:	No. That's totally clear right now—it's a picture.
Scott:	Scan the circle.
Tony:	I'm feeling complete right now.
Scott:	Right, but scan the circle again.

Tony: Now I see this work, this inquiry, and I want to use it all the time. I can see myself using it to seek something in the future.

Scott: "I want to use this inquiry to seek something in the future." Are those words you, the incomplete person?

Tony: No, not at all. I saw how I wanted to use this inquiry for my own story. Now I'm wondering what I would be seeking through the inquiry. Some different story?

Scott: Yes. The story always tells you that you're incomplete. It wants to complete itself, but it never can, because it's always a story of time continuously chasing the future. But the inquiry is not about seeking. It's a present looking into whether you can actually find an incomplete self. It's the belief in an incomplete self that results in seeking. Can you find the incomplete person as you sit here right now?

Tony: A flurry of seeking thoughts and energy is happening. It's not directed toward a specific thing. It's just a restlessness.

Scott: Are the words "A flurry of seeking thoughts and energy is happening" the incomplete you?

Tony: Yes. I feel that strong sensation of restlessness.

Scott: Relax. Let that energy be there, without labels. Is that energy the incomplete you?

Tony: [*long pause*] No. The restlessness just relaxes whenever I do nothing with it. But what arises is the thought *I really am incomplete, even though I can't find that self.*

Scott: Look right at the words "I really am incomplete, even though I can't find that self." Are the words you?

Tony: [*laughing*] No!

Scott: All words vanish when you look directly at them, unless some emotion or sensation arises along with them. That's what makes words sticky. It not only makes them feel true but also makes it seem that the words themselves are *you.* Can you find that incomplete you?

Tony: No, it's completely unfindable right now. It doesn't even feel like it's vaguely here. I feel invisible, but in a good way. So freeing!

Scott: Scan the circle again. Does it look like these things and people trigger you to seek?

Tony: No. There's no pull toward them at all now.

Scott: So who or what are you, really?

Tony: I can't even say I'm a complete person. That feels like a false story. It's like...storyless freedom or completion. That's the best I can do in trying to describe it.

More About Seeking

The kind of seeking described in this chapter is happening in our lives in so many ways that it can make our heads spin when we begin to look more closely at it. The Panorama Inquiry works well with useless seeking because it places all the people and things in our lives in a circle around us. By creating the circle, we can see that we are seeking in just about every direction.

Notice that when you rest in the moment, without emphasizing any thought, there is nothing to seek. There's nowhere to go. Here you are, in the present moment. Your thoughts have relaxed, and you're at peace. Even as you relax thoughts, you may notice that the energy in your body feels restless. Let that restless energy be as it is. Let it arise and fall without going back into the story of needing to seek something in the future, or from someone else. As the energy is allowed to relax, the mind relaxes with it more and more.

It's worth repeating that these inquiries are not designed to create another avenue for fruitless seeking. They aren't designed to get you something that you believe you lack. They're here to help you see through the self that lacks. That seeing through is always a *present* seeing. The inquiry brings you right back to where you already are, resting in the present moment. There's a stable well-being and contentment in presence. That sense of stable well-being and contentment is not based on getting to some later point, or getting something from someone else.

CHAPTER 18

Anxiety

Anxiety is often considered to be a condition that an individual suffers from, as if a person could exist in isolation, apart from relationships to other people and to things. If you suffer from anxiety, look at what's happening. There may be times when it feels as if you're anxious for no apparent reason. But much of the time, you're anxious about someone or something in your life that you have a relationship with—work, the future, death, illness, suffering, your coworkers, animals, crowds, germs, hospitals, or something or someone else. Looking at anxiety in the context of relationship can shed light on the core deficiency story that underlies the symptoms.

Using the Panorama Inquiry for Anxiety

Tamara: I suffer from anxiety.

Scott: About what?

Tamara: What do you mean, about what? It's a medical condition.

Scott: I realize that. But can you be anxious about nothing?

Tamara:	[*laughing*] No. I'm anxious about a lot of things.
Scott:	Put those things in a circle around you. What do these things bring up about you? Name that self.
Tamara:	Unsafe self.
Scott:	Scan the circle until anxiety comes up.
Tamara:	It's here. I see a future in which I won't be able to find a job.
Scott:	Is it a mental picture, words, or both?
Tamara:	Words.
Scott:	Are those words you, the unsafe self?
Tamara:	Yes.
Scott:	Stare at those words until they disappear. Feel the energy in your body. Is that energy you?
Tamara:	Yes.
Scott:	That means words or pictures are still arising. What are they?
Tamara:	I don't see any.
Scott:	Sometimes there's a picture of a body part, or an image of the body that's so subtle you don't see it at first.
Tamara:	I see it now. It's a tightly wound ball in my chest.
Scott:	Are the words "tightly wound ball in my chest" you?

Tamara:	No. Now it's just pure anxiety, with no picture.
Scott:	Are the words "it's just pure anxiety" you, the unsafe self?
Tamara:	No. I can see that I was still adding words to the energy.
Scott:	Feel the energy without words and pictures.
Tamara:	There's not much there without thoughts—just a buzzing energy.
Scott:	Are the words "just a buzzing energy" you?
Tamara:	No. Wow, now that energy is releasing…it's not a big deal when I'm not thinking about it.
Scott:	Scan the circle.
Tamara:	I'm afraid of hospitals. I see a hospital in the circle.
Scott:	Is that mental picture you?
Tamara:	No, but now I see myself lying in a hospital bed, unable to breathe.
Scott:	Are the words "I see myself lying in a hospital bed, unable to breathe" you, the unsafe self?
Tamara:	No, but the unsafe me is the one lying in the bed.
Scott:	That mental picture is you?
Tamara:	Yeah.

Scott:	Stare at that picture until it dissolves. Allow the energy to be as it is, without a story.
Tamara:	The picture of the ball isn't there. But I can see I want this energy to go away.
Scott:	"I want this energy to go away." Are those words you?
Tamara:	No. And, again, just buzzing energy. Not a big deal anymore. It's releasing.
Scott:	Scan the circle.
Tamara:	I'm afraid of dying. It's hard for me to breathe right now.
Scott:	Are the words "I'm afraid of dying" you, the unsafe self?
Tamara:	Not the words, no.
Scott:	How about "it's hard for me to breathe"?
Tamara:	No, it's the breathing that feels like the unsafe me.
Scott:	Experience the sensation of breathing, without words and pictures around it. Is that the unsafe self?
Tamara:	No, it's just breathing, and it's starting to be normal now.
Scott:	Scan the circle.
Tamara:	Nothing is triggering me.

Scott: Can you find the unsafe person here?

Tamara: No.

Scott: Whenever you feel anxious, imagine the circle
             again. Then stop focusing on those things and
             people in the circle. Turn your attention to the
             sense of an unsafe self. Then try to find it.

Tamara: I will.

Scott: Remember, you're almost always anxious in
             relation to someone or something. You can't feel
             like an unsafe self unless there's something that
             seems to threaten your safety.

Tamara: But what about basic physical safety, like not
             getting hit by a car?

Scott: Your body knows how to protect you, when that's
             what is needed. It will instinctively move out of
             the way of the car. What we're talking about here
             is the psychological belief that you're unsafe at
             the core. That's more like an identity, or story,
             not an instinctual movement to get out of the
             way of a car.

Tamara: Thank you so much. This goes deep!

CHAPTER 19

Envy

Envy comes in many varieties. Our envious thoughts can be accompanied by stinging emotions as we encounter others who have something we don't have, or who seem more successful, attractive, rich, powerful, knowledgeable, or important. These traits in others have a way of really triggering the core deficiency story in us.

In the following inquiry, Preston was doing a lot of outward pointing, blind to what was operating within himself. What made all the difference was just helping Preston refocus on himself, and on what was driving the outward pointing.

Using the Panorama Inquiry for Envy

Preston: I have this gut feeling about certain people I see as overly concerned with material wealth, or about people who parade around and show off their pretty wives and get lots of attention.

Scott: What kind of feeling?

Preston: I despise them.

Scott: Create a circle of the people who trigger you the most. Scan the circle. Who do you despise the most?

Preston: One particular guy seems to love money. People flock around him. I think it's disgusting and shallow how they suck up to him. He eats it up.

Scott: OK, that's what you think about him. I get it. When you stop pointing the finger outward at him and point it back at yourself instead, what do you see? How do you feel about yourself in comparison to him?

Preston: I don't see anything.

Scott: There can be a blind spot here. But there's some reason you're doing all that outward pointing. Does he bring up some sense that you're deficient, inadequate, invalid, or something like that?

Preston: The first thing I see is that I feel I'm much more humble about things like making money.

Scott: Is that really how you feel about yourself? Is there a bit of overcompensation going on here, as if you were having difficulty telling the truth about how you actually feel about yourself at the core? You came to me because you're humble?

Preston: [*laughing*] I guess not. I feel a bit envious of him. I've had to work hard for what little I have.

Scott: Now we're getting somewhere. What is it that he has that you feel you lack?

Preston:	He gets attention. He gets to have a lot of fun. He has a beautiful wife.
Scott:	Pin it down to one specific kind of deficient self so we can have a name for it. Fill in the blank: "There's something wrong with me. I lack…"
Preston:	Importance. I feel unimportant when I look at him.
Scott:	Let's try to find that unimportant self and see if that clears things up about how you see him. Are the words "I feel unimportant" you, the unimportant self?
Preston:	Right away I feel a big lump in my throat, and in my gut. So, yes.
Scott:	Are the words "I feel a big lump in my throat" you?
Preston:	Of course not. I'm just describing what came up.
Scott:	OK, stop describing the sensation in your throat. Just sit here with me, resting, without words to describe that sensation. Do you see a picture of your throat in your mind's eye?
Preston:	Yes.
Scott:	Is that picture you, the unimportant self?
Preston:	I have to say yes. For some reason, it feels like that's me.
Scott:	Are the words "it feels like that's me" you?

Preston: No. It's so subtle. The mind is so subtle. I didn't see that the voice in my head was actually attaching those words to that picture.

Scott: Rest. Just notice the open space of the present moment. Feel its expansiveness. Feel the alive space within the body. Now, do you see that picture?

Preston: It just fell away. And the lump fell away, too.

Scott: Where is the self that's unimportant?

Preston: I see his face.

Scott: Is that picture of his face you, the unimportant self?

Preston: There's a charge to it, so—yes.

Scott: Can you let that picture fade for a few seconds and feel the emotion or sensation that arose with it?

Preston: Yes. I feel sad.

Scott: Are the words "I feel sad" you?

Preston: No.

Scott: Sit with the sadness, without labeling it. Let that energy expand into the space.

Preston: I feel a great resistance to doing that.

Scott: Are those words you?

Preston: No.

Scott:	You can probably see now why you were doing all that outward pointing—so you wouldn't have to feel this inner sadness. Feel it now, but without describing it.
Preston:	[*crying*] This is embarrassing. But somehow it feels good. I feel a release.
Scott:	The energy that's releasing—is that the unimportant you?
Preston:	No.
Scott:	Can you find the unimportant you as you rest, letting words, pictures, and energies arise and fall naturally?
Preston:	Some of the thoughts seem like me until I just look right at them, and then they fall away. No, I can't find that self.
Scott:	Scan the circle again. Who triggers you?
Preston:	I'm not getting a trigger from him anymore, but now I see my wife being extra nice to this guy who does plumbing work for us. I despise him, too.
Scott:	Are the words "I despise him" you, the one who's not important?
Preston:	No.
Scott:	How about the mental picture of your wife being nice to him?

Preston:	No. It feels like I'm the one watching all that. The unimportant person is watching her do that.
Scott:	Are the words "I'm watching her do that" the unimportant you?
Preston:	No, but the words seem to point to me.
Scott:	When you drop the words, can you find the *me* that the words point to?
Preston:	Feels like someone sucker-punched me in the gut.
Scott:	Are those words you?
Preston:	No.
Scott:	Rest without those words, and feel the sensation in the gut.
Preston:	It feels really stuck.
Scott:	Are those words you?
Preston:	No. I can see that my mind just wants to come back in and describe everything.
Scott:	Are any of those descriptions the unimportant you?
Preston:	No. Again, it feels like they point to me.
Scott:	Find that *me*.
Preston:	It's in my gut.
Scott:	Is that description you?
Preston:	No. OK—I get it. Let me sit with the actual pain instead of describing it [*long pause*]. The sensation

turned to sadness, and now, as I'm letting that sadness expand, without words, it seems to diminish.

Scott: Is that diminishing energy you?

Preston: No.

Scott: Scan the circle.

Preston: Oh, this is weird. I see my mother paying more attention to my brother than to me as a kid.

Scott: Is that picture you?

Preston: Yes. But I'm resting and letting the feeling be there. Let me have a moment [*sobbing*]. God, I feel like I've been left out of everything in life.

Scott: Are those words you?

Preston: They're just words.

Scott: Remember, we're not here just trying to rehash the past or psychoanalyze you. We're doing something very specific—trying to find the self that is unimportant. Can you find that? Look everywhere.

Preston: None of the thoughts feel like that self. It's this body. There's something wrong with this body. I'm not attractive.

Scott: Look at the words you just said. Picture them in a frame in your mind. Stare right at the words. Are those words you, the unimportant self?

Preston: No.

Scott: Can you find it?

Preston: I feel completely relaxed right now. No, I can't find it.

Scott: Scan the circle. Are you triggered?

Preston: No—just a mild sensation or emotion here and there. They're not the unimportant self. What an incredible story I've been secretly telling myself!

Scott: It results in a lot of outward pointing, doesn't it?

Preston: Hell yes! It was really unintelligent to do all that pointing when the issue was really with me, with this sense of being unimportant.

Scott: Don't beat yourself up. The sense of deficiency is a common human story. Just stick to seeing if you can find that self here.

Preston: I can't find it.

Scott: Now look back at all those others. Is there really anything wrong with them?

Preston: No, they just are who they are. This was all about me. They look perfect. I don't despise them. I despised myself—I can see that.

Scott: Are the words "I despised myself" the unimportant you?

Preston: [laughing] No.

CHAPTER 20

Jealousy

Jealousy is similar to envy, but there is a critical difference. Jealousy involves the fear of losing something or someone valuable. If a husband flirts with another woman, his wife is not really envious of the other woman. She is experiencing jealousy, which is fear of losing her husband. This fear strikes at the very core of her sense of self-worth.

It's because of this fear that we sometimes experience a very intense reaction to the prospect of losing someone valuable to us. Our sense of self-worth is dependent on that person. If the person strays, then the fear of loss surfaces and creates an intense response in us.

Using the Boomerang Inquiry for Jealousy

Frank: My wife works for a dentist who's very attractive
           and charming. They have lunch together
           regularly. She often talks about him in very
           endearing ways. I know that this is how marriages
           often end—through affairs that start at work.

Scott: What is your wife mirroring back to you about
           your own perceived deficiency?

Frank:	Well, I thought we would focus the inquiry on the dentist, since my anger is mostly directed toward him.
Scott:	Let's start with your wife and see where that goes.
Frank:	I'm angry at her, too.
Scott:	That's the outward pointing. But point the finger back at yourself. What is she mirroring back about you?
Frank:	When she talks about him with that sparkle in her eye, I get furious and afraid she'll leave.
Scott:	That's good. Those are the emotions. And those emotions result in the outward pointing. But what do the emotions seem to say about you—about how you're deficient in some way?
Frank:	I feel less attractive and charming than he is. It's as if there are some important parts that I wasn't born with, and he got them all.
Scott:	Reduce all that down to a specific self.
Frank:	I'm insignificant.
Scott:	Can you find that insignificant self right now?
Frank:	Ugh! Yes. Pit of my stomach.
Scott:	Are the words "pit of my stomach" the insignificant self?
Frank:	No, but it feels like that self is *in* the pit of my stomach.

Scott:	Are those words you?
Frank:	No.
Scott:	Then actually look into the pit of your stomach. What do you see or feel?
Frank:	There's a black hole there.
Scott:	Are the words "black hole" you, the insignificant person?
Frank:	I know they're just words, but they carry such an intense response. So, yes!
Scott:	Relax all words and pictures, and look right at that black hole. What do you see?
Frank:	It's a really dark area that feels as solid as a rock.
Scott:	Look at the picture your mind is projecting into your gut, but without describing that picture. Is that picture you, the insignificant self?
Frank:	Well, it doesn't look like it's me now. It looks like something I'm looking at.
Scott:	So you see that there's an awareness looking at the picture?
Frank:	Yes.
Scott:	Rest, and let the picture just be there, but without attaching any words to it. Is that awareness the insignificant self?
Frank:	That's a funny question. I thought you were going to ask if that *picture* is the self. No,

awareness is just aware. It's not insignificant or significant. It's not really any story at all.

Scott: Don't skip over that seeing. Soak it in.

Frank: Yes, that's peaceful—knowing myself as that space. But now the picture of the dentist is coming up, and it feels like I'm insignificant. Happens so quickly!

Scott: That mental picture of him—is that you, the insignificant self? Look right at the picture, but notice that it's within this clear, open space of awareness.

Frank: Yes. I feel rage toward him when I see that picture.

Scott: Let the picture come to rest by looking right at it as it dissolves. Then look at the word "rage." Is that word you?

Frank: No. I'm just using that word to describe this intense feeling.

Scott: Take a moment, and rest, without describing that intense feeling. Take your time. Let that energy be there as it is.

Frank: When I stop describing it, it relaxes. The energy is not me. I can see that.

Scott: Where is the insignificant self?

Frank: Nowhere. There are some subtle pictures and words, but nothing feels like me. It's all moving through, and I'm just watching it come and go.

Scott:	Look back at your wife. When you see her, does that trigger the sense that you're insignificant?
Frank:	Sadness comes up. This feels like the genuine emotion behind all this. The rage was covering it up.
Scott:	The *word* "sadness" covers up the actual *energy* of sadness. Rest, and allow that energy to be, without attaching any words to it. Is that energy you?
Frank:	Yes.
Scott:	That just means words and pictures are still arising. Just notice what's arising, but don't follow the words and pictures. Let the sadness fly by in the same way a bird flies through the air, without leaving any trace.
Frank:	Ahhh…the sadness almost feels nice, like it's turning into a warm sensation.
Scott:	Is that sensation you, the insignificant self?
Frank:	It feels good—but, no, it's not an insignificant self.
Scott:	Can you find the insignificant self?
Frank:	No. It's not here. Each time I see something come up, it just falls away into that open space.

More About Pointing Outward

Jealousy is a good topic to use when we want to explore how pointing outward serves as a way of dealing with inner pain.

That's because jealousy can bring up an intense desire to point outward.

Imagine a man whose index finger is pointing outward at everyone else. With his energy focused outward, he's blind to his painful feelings, and his outward pointing is also keeping him from seeing that he believes in a core deficient self, an empty self from which he's doing all this outward pointing. He won't be able to experience his emotions directly, without words and pictures, until he can begin to relax and let those emotions just be as they are.

The source of our pain always looks like another person. For Frank, the sources of his pain looked like his wife and the dentist she worked for. But Frank, by focusing inward, was able to see the insignificant self as empty, and that transformation changed the way he related both to his pain and to his wife. Because he discovered the open spaciousness within him, and the unfindability of the core deficient self, Frank was now in a better position to be honest about his own feelings instead of trying to deflect them by focusing outward in blame and rage. He was able to see through the insignificant self. But that didn't mean he couldn't express his concerns to his wife. He could still say, "Honey, I think you're getting a bit too close to your boss." He and his wife could then engage in a mature conversation about the feelings that had come up in Frank in reaction to his wife's admiration of her boss.

Clearly, all Frank's outward pointing had brought him little resolution or healing; otherwise he wouldn't have come to me in the first place. And sometimes it does take years of pointing outward before we see that it doesn't work—pointing outward doesn't heal us, and it doesn't resolve the conflicts in our relationships. Chances are that Frank had tried to speak to his wife about this matter, but that he'd spoken from the pain instead of facing it. By not facing the pain, he remained blind to the insignificant self, his core sense of deficiency. When we're blind to how the core deficient self drives our emotions and our actions, we become caught in a constant loop of turning away from our own pain and focusing on the actions of others. But when we become willing to face the core wounds within us, we can finally engage in authentic communication.

The Middle Way in Relationship

Our language is dualistic—*you and I, self and other*—a web of opposites. When you believe its every word, it seems to present life to you as it really is. Our dualistic language implies strict separation between people, and between objects. That belief in separation is exactly what is released through the inquiries presented in this book.

Words cannot truly describe what is realized when you see through the sense of separation and the story of the core deficient self. So don't just read this book and then close it. If you do, you'll never have more than an intellectual understanding of what's known as the *Middle Way*, and it may seem confusing and perhaps even contradictory to you.

What Is the Middle Way?

The Middle Way is where you're free from two extreme views— the view that everything is separate, and the view that nothing exists. It's where you see through separation and deficiency while retaining an appreciation for the diversity of *appearances*, the ever-shifting play of what appears to be me, you, us, them, the world.

In the Middle Way, you don't pretend that nothing exists. The play of life is always going on, and the play of relationship appears within it. Things and people still appear to be there in the Middle Way, and yet they can't be found as concrete, objective, separate entities. Instead, they assume a non-fixed, non-objective quality, showing up by way of the words, pictures, and energies that arise to paint them into your experience in certain ways. As the strict sense of a separate self and a separate other relaxes, people and things appear more and more empty. Self and other, like all opposites, are experienced as mirages, as if they were reflections on the surface of a pond, where no individual reflection on the water's surface can be grasped as a concrete object, and where no one reflection seems separated from the others, although each one retains its individual uniqueness. Communication takes on a lightness and ease as you see that you experience other people as a play of words, pictures, and energies, all by way of a filter that is unique to you. You also see the reverse—that when others relate to and communicate with you, they experience you through their own subjective filters.

Once you've seen through separation, you find a natural peace, compassion, love, and ease of being with others in the Middle Way, whether you're talking together or resting together in silence. Now you can use language for practical purposes, and as a way to communicate. It's an intelligent tool—there's no need to make it into an enemy. Language is no longer a problem when you're not using it to define your self as inherently separate and deficient. Ideas swirl around, but they don't belong to anyone. They don't land anywhere. They come and they go, leaving no trace behind. And you can enjoy being with others in silence, a profound quiet in which thought doesn't arise much at all, and in which there's a profound knowing of *Oneness*, a present awareness of deep intimacy and complete unity between and among all things, all people, all countries, all political views, all perspectives. When you're with others in silence, fully present in the moment, you aren't processing life through the linguistic, dualistic web of opposites. You can find it very sweet and intimate to be with others in this way, the Middle Way.

In the Middle Way, life is relationship. Everything is interconnected. Separation no longer makes sense, and it's no longer your experience. And yet, even as you see through separation, deficiency, and objectivity, you retain your unique, subjective view of things, a view influenced by your history, your thoughts, your feelings, your culture, and your family upbringing. All these influences continue to operate in you as long as you're speaking and thinking.

The mind is like a computer that picks up information. That information, once processed, becomes the subjective filter through which you experience others and the world of things. Individual viewpoints still arise, but they're naturally held more lightly, apart from any need to create a sense of "self" and "other" out of them. You retain the capacity to speak your mind and take whatever action feels authentic to you. For example, you can move in and out of different relationships, and you can leave a relationship that is abusive or that no longer works for you. When you use the inquiries to look for triggers in relationship, you're able to remain open to seeing how your subjective filter comes to be taken for reality itself.

A Final Word About the Inquiries

The best way to experience what is realized when you see through the sense of separation and the story of the core deficient self, and the best way to understand how that realization benefits relationship, is to use the inquiries. If they seem a bit daunting at first, have patience. They become easier to use as you delve into them.

If you can, start by working with a trained facilitator. When someone else is asking you the questions, it's easier for you to look at the words, pictures, and energies that are arising within you. A facilitator guides you slowly, holds the space for you, and helps you keep from overcomplicating the process. But you don't have to find a facilitator before you can start using the inquiries. As we've seen, people can benefit from using the inquiries on their own.

Couples can use the inquiries together, too. In fact, people in any kind of relationship—friends, parents and children, brothers and sisters—can benefit from using the inquiries with each other. It can be enlightening to see what the people closest to you really believe about themselves, and this kind of shared exploration creates an atmosphere of compassion, vulnerability, and transparency. It's wonderful if the people close to you are also doing the inquiries presented in this book, since the belief in objectivity is released for you as well as for them, and what is created is a peace and harmony that must be experienced to be fully appreciated. But the inquiries are for *you*. If you're interacting with people who are not interested in releasing the belief in separation, deficiency, and objectivity, and if you're finding those interactions to be a challenge, then you'll also find that the inquiries are a perfect tool for discovering how you're buying into separation in your relationships with those people. When you clean up your side of the street, it's hard to see anything wrong with someone else's side. Others are as they are, and you'll be aware of their subjective filters, even if they remain unaware of them. Once you've seen through your own subjective filter, it's impossible not to be aware of how those filters operate in others.

As you learn how the inquiries work, they become a part of you for a while. They become second nature, and you're able to use them more and more quickly and easily. You're likely to reach the point where you can simply look at a thought, a mental picture, or an energy and ask, "Is this me?" And you'll immediately see that what you're looking at is just a thought or a picture or an energy, not a self, and it will fall away. As the inquiries become second nature, this seeing becomes even more immediate, and you come to recognize, instantly, that words, pictures, and energies never form a separate, deficient self. The core deficiency story is immediately seen through, and the deficient self is seen to be empty and unfindable. The core deficiency story may stop arising altogether, but even if it continues to arise, it will become just another opportunity for you to see, in the moment, that no self is really formed. There are only words, pictures, and energies that appear and then disappear without a trace.

Working with the Boomerang Inquiry and the Panorama Inquiry, you'll come to see the mirror of relationship everywhere you look, and yet you won't feel trapped by it. You'll see that whenever you express a view, its opposite is automatically implied. *Self* implies *other*, *us* implies *them*, *black* implies *white*, *deficient* implies *non-deficient*, *worthy* implies *unworthy*—you'll no longer mistake these things and ideas for identities that exist in strict isolation, apart from their opposites and apart from the words, pictures, and energies arising within you.

As you use the inquiries, the mind clears. Thoughts, when they arise, are quieter and more transparent. You no longer mistake them for who or what you are. And as the mind clears, the heart area begins to open on its own. This opening of the heart comes about organically as you see that separation is never your experience, and neither is deficiency. You feel emotions more immediately, as soon as they arise, with no need to label them or identify with them. They come and go more quickly, and they're no longer hooked into a core story of separation and deficiency. The body feels more vibrant, alive, open, spacious, and peaceful, and the more you rest your attention in the area of your heart, the more open and welcoming your heart becomes to whatever appears in your present experience.

Remember, though, that using the inquiries is not about seeking in vain for objects or other people to provide what your self seems to lack. Nor is using the inquiries about achieving self-improvement, gaining enlightenment, or creating a better version of your core story. It's about resting in the Middle Way—organically, in the moment—as you experience a natural freedom from belief in a separate, deficient self. Selflessness is seen to be your natural state, and relationship is no longer a source of suffering, seeking, or conflict.

Acknowledgments

This book was truly a labor of love. Thanks to all the people in my life, too many to name, who acted as teachers and reflected back to me my own core deficiency story so I could see through it. Special thanks to Curt King, Fiona Robertson, Julianne Eanniello, and Chad Sewich.

Scott Kiloby is a noted author, teacher, and international speaker on the subject of non-dual wisdom as it applies to addiction, depression, anxiety, and trauma. He is founder of a worldwide community of Living Inquiries facilitators who work with people in over twelve different countries. He is also cofounder of The Kiloby Center for Recovery in Rancho Mirage, CA, the first addiction, anxiety, and depression treatment center to focus primarily on mindfulness.

MORE BOOKS from NON-DUALITY PRESS

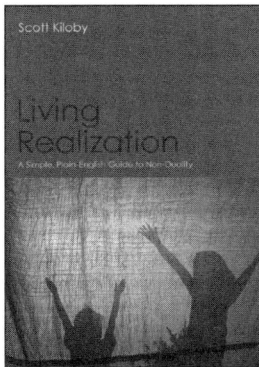

Scott Kiloby

Living Realization
A Simple, Plain-English Guide to Non-Duality

ISBN: 978-1908664464 | US $13.95

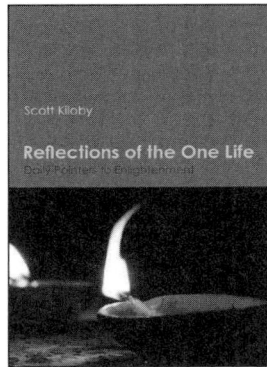

Scott Kiloby

Reflections of the One Life
Daily Pointers to Enlightenment

ISBN: 978-1908664471 | US $19.95

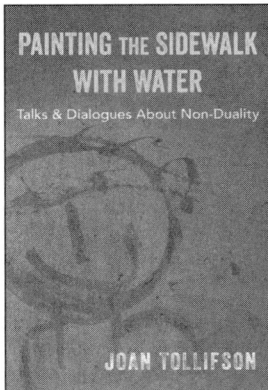

PAINTING THE SIDEWALK WITH WATER
Talks & Dialogues About Non-Duality

JOAN TOLLIFSON

ISBN: 978-0956643216 | US $19.95

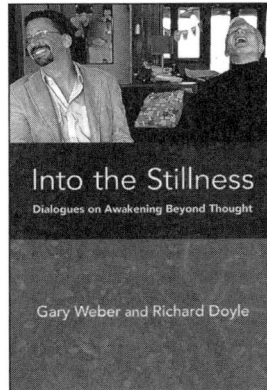

Into the Stillness
Dialogues on Awakening Beyond Thought

Gary Weber and Richard Doyle

ISBN: 978-1908664532 | US $16.95

NON-DUALITY PRESS
An Imprint of New Harbinger Publications
www.newharbinger.com